SLOWING *Time*

BARBARA MAHANY

SLOWING
Time

SEEING
the SACRED
OUTSIDE YOUR
KITCHEN
DOOR

ABINGDON PRESS
NASHVILLE

SLOWING TIME
SEEING THE SACRED OUTSIDE YOUR KITCHEN DOOR

Copyright © 2014 by Barbara Mahany

All rights reserved.

Library of Congress Cataloging-in-Publication Data

Mahany, Barbara.
  Slowing time : seeing the sacred outside your kitchen door / Barbara Mahany.
    pages cm
  Includes bibliographical references.
  1. Meditations. 2. Spiritual life--Christianity. I. Title.
  BV4832.3.M3175 2014
  242--dc23

                                                              2014028804

ISBN 978-1-4267-7642-7

13 14 15 16 17 18 19 20 21 22--10 9 8 7 6 5 4 3 2 1

MANUFACTURED IN THE UNITED STATES OF AMERICA

For my boys—Blair, Will, Teddy—holy trinity,
infinite wonder; and Blair, ever, for believing

For my mama, the Original Mother Nature

For my papa, Lumen, never extinguished . . .

And for my "chair" sisters, none by birth, all by heart

Praying

It doesn't have to be

the blue iris, it could be

weeds in a vacant lot, or a few

small stones; just

pay attention, then patch

a few words together and don't try

to make them elaborate, this isn't

a contest but the doorway

into thanks, and a silence in which

another voice may speak.

—Mary Oliver

Winter

Season of Deepening

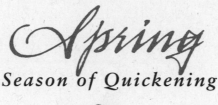

Spring

Season of Quickening

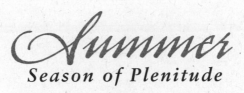

Summer

Season of Plenitude

Autumn
Season of Awe

Winter
Season of Stillness

A NOTE FROM MY KITCHEN TABLE

AT ITS HEART, THIS IS A BOOK OF WONDER. Of beholding the every-day miracle. Of wrapping our arms around the Holy Within and the Holy All Around.

Consider this a field guide. To wonder, certainly, and wisdom, perhaps. It borrows, in spirit, from the almanac, the scrapbook, scribbled field notes, assorted jottings, and, on occasion, the banged-up recipe file that's tucked on my kitchen shelf.

It's a book I hope you come to know as something of a friend, a gentle-souled companion you might choose to cozy up with— on a porch swing, in your comfy chair, or under your snuggliest bedcovers.

It unfurls month by month, season upon season.

I have long been enchanted, enraptured by the miracle of this holy Earth's turning, its invitation to follow the circle of the year, the depth of winter, quickening of spring, plenitude of summer, autumnal awe. And to discover, back to winter once again, that really it's a spiral; while the world around has echoes of the famil-iar—from the slant of winter's light, to the particular nip in the air—who we are deep inside is ever ripening, hardly the same one winter to the next.

I pay attention—in this book, and in my every day—to the

senses, those receptors of the human vessel that bring us in communion with all that's holy. If we're keen to their whisper, they're the channels to the still, small voice that stirs within—awaiting, always waiting.

Stitched through the seasons and the months ahead, you'll find bits and snippets—French knots and patchwork squares, I like to think—of whole-body enticements to enter into the bounty of the calendar. The enticement might be a summons to unfurl a blanket—on the fire escape or in a meadow—to settle in for a night of stargazing or an afternoon's cloud parade. Or a ladle from the cookstove, served up in a recipe that captures a season's depth and deliciousness.

The aim, at every turn, is to hold the holy hour up to the light. Extract the essence, the marrow, the deep-down glory, and the everyday gospel.

These pages, I pray, will be a springboard for your own meandering into the Holy. Because I'm Christian—specifically, Catholic—and my husband is Jewish, our family encounters the Divine in the rituals and idioms of two faith traditions. I've found, over time, that the dual lenses refract and magnify both light and shadow, and that my sense of the sacred pulses through the year.

Month by month, season upon season, we march through time. We choose: Savor—savor it all, every blessed morsel. Or let it slip away, unnoticed, unrecognized for the majesty, the miracle, each moment offers.

Pay close attention, is the beckoning. Behold the Holy Hours.

Winter
Season of Deepening

WINTER (OR DECEMBER) SOLSTICE

---

*The new year begins a quarter moon after winter's opening
curtain. And winter, at least in the Northern Hemisphere,
opens with the December solstice. In short, the solstice
brings on the longest night—up north, anyway. At its essence,
solstice science is plain-angled geometry: The winter solstice
comes at the very moment the North Pole is tilted farthest
from the sun. The shadow cast is never longer. Nor, the night.
In the Southern Hemisphere, it's flipped: short shadow, short
night, summer light, with the South Pole tilted nearest the
sun; the poetic symmetry of heaven and Earth. Depending on
where on the globe you happen to be, the solstice falls on or
near December 21.*

WINTER'S WONDERLIST

———❧❧❧———

it's the season of . . .

snow-laden sky creeping in unawares . . .

the red-cheeked badge of courage, come the close of a slow-spooled walk through winter's woods . . .

frost ferns on the windowpanes . . .

snow falling first in feather-tufts, then fairy-dusted stars, and, finally, prodigiously, in what could only be curds . . .

noses pressed to glass, keeping watch as winter's storm wallops . . .

soup kettle murmuring—slow, steady, hungrily . . .

pinecones crackling in the hearth . . .

mittens that dare to be lost, lest they're tethered to strings knotted and threaded through coat sleeves . . .

scribble your own here:

A Count-Your-Blessings Calendar:
Blessed Be Winter,
Season of Deepening

In the Christian liturgical calendar the year opens amid the twelve days of Christmas, not long after the Nativity. In distant darkness, the brightest star blinks on, drawing the wisest journeyers. Epiphany. And so unfold the depths of Christmastide. In the Hebrew calendar, it won't be long till Tu B'Shevat, the Jewish new year of the trees, when, in mid-winter in Israel, the almond tree awakes from its winter's slumber, and sixteenth-century Jewish mystics taught that we elevate ourselves by partaking of seven new-year fruits. If eaten with holy intention, we're told, sparks of light hidden inside the fruits' soft flesh will be broken open and freed to float to heaven, completing the circle of life's renewal. The long dark weeks of winter wend, for Christians, into Ordinary Time, until Lent begins, and with it the hope of purification, of burning away, cleansing, all that keeps us from holiness through and through.

Here, fourteen blessings to stitch into your winter hours, blueprints for beholding the Holy, practicing the art of paying supreme attention. Some are tied to particular dates, others might be sprinkled throughout the season, for homegrown encounters with the wonder-filled.

NEW YEAR'S DAY (JAN. 1): *Usher in the new year with a day of quietude; sunrise to sundown, hushed. Unplug. Slow simmer. Amble. May the loudest utterance be the turning of a page. Or the murmur of a tender kiss.*

BLESSING 2: *Weather lesson: In life, we are wise to keep ourselves stocked deep inside with whatever it takes to weather all that life throws our way. It is resilience with which we must line our inner shelves. And unswerving faith, stored in gallon jugs, to ride out any storm.*

EPIPHANY (JAN. 6): *Bundle up and take a moonwalk. Consider the gift of the nightlight that waxes and wanes but always guides our way. Pay attention to the moon's portion. Keep a moon journal, recording each night's lunar fraction, on the way toward wholeness or decline. What blessing, especially for a child. Isn't this the miracle of learning to marvel?*

BLESSING 4: *There is something mystical about the drama of a winter storm. You can't help but feel small as the sky turns marbled gray, the winds pick up, howl. Trees commence their thrashing. It's a fine thing for the human species to remember the amplitude of what we're up against.*

Rev. Dr. Martin Luther King Jr.'s Birthday

(Jan. 15): *Read the whole of Dr. King's "I Have a Dream" speech. Picture the world as you would dream it, then set out to make it real, one act of kindness at a time.*

Blessing 6: *Take extra care to scatter cracked corn, peanut butter-smeared pine cones, and suet cakes for the loyal backyard critters who've settled in for winter, especially when arctic winds screech. Whisper thanks for those who keep watch on us.*

Blessing 7: *Proffer consecration for the scarlet-cloaked cardinal—the one flash of pigment till Valentines flutter. He is the very heartbeat of promise, hope on a wing, a laugh-out-loud reminder that we are not alone. That red of reds shatters all that's bleak, shouts: "There is life where you are doubting."*

Candlemas (Feb. 2):

Amid the winter's darkness, pause to consider the blessing of the candles, ordained to illuminate the hours. Fill your kitchen table, gathering a flock of orphan candlesticks. Adorn with winter branches and berries clinging to the bough.

BLESSING 9: *Behold the hush of snowfall. The flakes free-falling past the porch light, their hard-angled intricacies and puffy contours tumbling, tumbling, lulling all the world and its weary citizens into that fugue state that comes with heavy snow—when at last we take in breath, and hold it. Fill our empty lungs.*

BLESSING 10: *Be dazzled by the diamond-dusted world you just woke up to. The way the flakes catch bits of moonlight, shimmer like a thousand million stars. To be dazzled is a prayer.*

VALENTINE'S DAY (FEB. 14): *Tuck love notes under pillows, inside lunch bags and coat pockets. Sprinkle a trail of construction-paper hearts from bedside to breakfast table, and christen the day with whimsies and joy. Murmur deep thanks for the gifts of heart.*

BLESSING 12: *Sometimes winter pushes us to the ends of our hope. It can be the season of nearly giving up. But then the holy hallelujah comes—the red bird, the pure contentment of mere survival, the steaming bowl of soup when you come in from shoveling, winter's Sisyphean folly.*

BLESSING 13: *Savor the sanctuary of being tucked in a cozy kitchen, looking out at a winter world of which we stand in awe. Bless the contemplative nature of this season that draws us into the depths of our cave, where we find fuel for the seasons still to come.*

BLESSING 14: *Bundle up for a meandering walk in the end-of-winter woods, marvel at the survival of so many species. Marvel at your own.*

FRESH START
On Ascending

BY ACCIDENT OF BIRTH, I CAME ONTO THE PLANET on the third day of a new year, and so all my life—and especially of late—I dwell in my own personal calendar of time delay. The beauty of this stalled beginning is that I've extra hours to contemplate the fresh start. To consider hard and deep just how I might aim to live this year.

I am fueled by aims—a walking, talking, I'll-do-better machine.

And on this gray morning, this morning laced in shadow, my humble vows begin with the quotidian: My shortlist bull's-eyes my knack for piddling away my appointed hours. I'm tackling the humdrum here before I take on the herculean, the stuff that truly might amount to wholesale revolution of the soul.

It's the way—morning after morning, bedtime after bedtime—I rush my little fellow, always chiming that we're late, we're late. Next, it's the homespun fears that keep me locked inside my comfort zone, too full of cockamamie worries to tread beyond my

January Field Notes: Full Wolf Moon, sometimes called Old Moon or Moon after Yule, shines down on a sliver of January's

self-conscribed borders. And, third, the certain shyness that stops me from broadly spreading my wings.

These would be among the litany of my daily sins. Yet, there's consolation and it comes with a knowing that offers deliverance:

Deep in the truth of all of us lies the rough draft that demands edit after edit.

And so we are blessed, those of us who keep time, who trace the day, the week, the year in spiral.

It is, at heart, a geometry of promise, hope, and, most of all, ascension. It offers us the chance, over and over, to come back to that sacred moment when we stand at the crest of the hill, cast arms wide, salute the heavens, shake off dirt and dust, remap our route, and see if this time 'round we might inch higher toward the summit.

I don't know a world religion that doesn't devote a chapter, at least, to absolution, cleansing, rinsing. It is as if we are hard-wired for holy resurrection. To rise from our brokenness. To seek forgiveness for our sins and shortcomings. To come back to the fresh start, the blank slate, to try and try again. To believe in the almighty "take two."

And so it is that I come on bended knee. I stand here praying, hoping, promising that my next go-around on this old globe might be one that draws me closer to the unfettered essence I was meant to be. The one not weighted down with doubt and double-guessing. The one that drinks in all the holy waters all around me.

---

days. Back when Native Americans were pinning names to each month's brightest lunar light, wolf packs howled hungrily outside

It is, I hope and pray and believe, by little and by little—by little dose of courage, by little kindness, by little gentleness—that we inhale the promise: to shake off our wobbles, stand tall, and launch the climb again.

At the start of this new year, it's what I whisper. And what sets me on my way.

---

the villages, amid the new year's frigid cold and snow. Orion, the great hunter, rules the night sky. Sunlight, in these nascent weeks

INVITING IN THE SACRED
On Absorbing the Holy

SOMEONE ASKED ME NOT SO LONG AGO why I search so often for the sacred in my every day.

It's not so much the searching, really, it's that I often seem to stumble on it. Or maybe it exerts a pull, and I can't steer away.

It's just there.

I find it, often, tucking little ones to bed. Or sitting side by side on stools carved by my brother, in that after-school ebb and flow, when the third-grade day comes rushing out in breathless narrative, and, every paragraph or so, in goes a bite of apple, or cookie, or glug of chocolate milk.

I do, yes, find the sacred nearly every time I tiptoe out the door. Not the times when I'm near a gallop, racing to the station wagon, keys clunking from my fist, late—too often—for where I was supposed to be a good ten minutes ago. But in the tiptoe times, when every pore of me is wide awake and at attention, when I'm in slow gear, trying not to barrel through, disturb the

---

*just after the longest night, grows by the day, minute upon minute added to the dawn and the twilight. * Deep beneath the earth,*

peace. Then it's almost certain that the sacred will alight on me, as a monarch to a black-eyed Susan.

I find the Holy Breath in birdsong, absolutely. And in the streams of light pouring through the pines, or the crack in the fence that runs along my cottage garden.

I find knee-dropping humility when I spy the moon. Or when, weeks behind schedule, a vine I thought had died breaks out in bloom, a resurrection lesson every time.

I find God whenever I'm alone. Or maybe that's the time when, at last, I feel the rustling by my side, at my elbow, where my heart goes thump. Maybe that's when at last it's quiet enough, still enough, for me to hear the Holy Whispers.

I do know that God spends time aplenty in my kitchen, at my dinner table. I sink my fists into the egg-rich dough of the challah in the making, and I hear the prayers take off. I dump cinnamon and raisins in a pot of bubbling porridge, and, voilà, I am at one with the heartbeat of all the saints and angels who've passed this way, who've known what it is to be called to care for others as if their blessed mother.

At every meal when we join hands, a circle of palms touching palms, fingers wrapped around fingers, I feel a veil of holiness drop down upon us. Especially so when we've invited in a friend or stranger we'd not known so well before.

Egad, I even find the sacred scrubbing out the tub. Not always. But sometimes. Folding clothes. Turning on the iron, smoothing out the wrinkles.

Isn't that, at the heart of it, what the sacred brings?

bulbs slumber but stirring begins as the scape (or stalk) stretches, and stores of sustenance undergird resurrection, come longer,

An otherworldly way of living on a higher plane?

Isn't this all just molecules and space between if there's no purpose to the plan? Aren't we merely moving markers round the game board, passing through the stations, checking off the list, if there's no Teacher, no Comforter, no Great Illuminator?

Oh, you needn't call it by a single name. Nor pray a certain prayer.

All I'm thinking here is that to tap into the sacred, to invite it in your home, your heart, your rushing to the train, or your talking to the grocery checker, is to take it up a notch. To infuse the beautiful and the breathtaking into the simple act of breaking bread and sipping wine. Or stirring soup. Or whispering in a child's ear, "Don't be afraid. I'm here."

Isn't all of life just a long equation of simple addition and subtraction? Don't we make it into poetry, geometry, by seeing it through a lens that understands, at the heart of every breath, every word, every triumphant act of courage, every heart-crushing blow, that we are not here merely by the power of our own two legs?

But that there are wings all around, holding us afloat, wrapping us, taking us on a sacred flight to everlasting truth and holy wisdom.

That's why I seem to stumble on the sacred.

I don't think I'd stay upright otherwise.

---

*deeper daylight. * Cardinals, the scarlet-feathered flock, are first ones to the feeder shortly after daybreak, and last ones headed to*

TEACHING TO SEE
On Paying Attention

THE LESSON: HOW TO REGARD. HOW TO WATCH. How to take in the world.

Here's how it unfolded: I bounded the stairs, breathless—and ten minutes late—to roust my little one from his sheets.

He rolled out of bed the way he usually does: somersault off the pillow to sprawled on his back at the end of the mattress, head dangling, flopping like some sort of upside-down rag doll, not too far from the ground. A perfect inverted perch, he decided, for keeping watch out the window.

That's when he announced, "Papa is out on the roof. He's hopping around. I think maybe he's looking for breakfast."

Papa is the red bird, papa cardinal, a character around here who goes by only one name.

After broadcasting every breath Papa was taking out there on the roof, just below the window through which he was watching, my little one reached for the ledge, grabbed the binoculars.

---

*the nest at nightfall. * Off in the woods, Great Horned Owls carry on the timeless rites of wingspread coupling, a not-so-delicate*

Suddenly, the boy hanging there with his curls topsy-turvy wanted to learn how to look through the little glass circles that, through the wizardry of optics alone, bring the world as close as the end of your nose.

As I tried—it's clumsier than you might imagine—to line up the eye pieces, tried to narrow then widen the space between so they fit to his face, as he attempted to make the looking all clear, not blurry, not too close, not too far, not staring down at the gutter, but trying to get that old bird in his lens, I realized, really, I was teaching the boy how to see.

How to regard. How to watch. How to take in the world without any words.

How to notice the pinhole there on the side of Papa's small beak. How to study the feathers he fluffs when it's cold. How to see the ballet of flurries and ice on the boughs as they shudder there in the deep winter's wind.

He was, for a while, finding it hard. The bird was nowhere in sight. All he saw were the nail heads there on the shingles. Not quite the subject of choice for "Intro to Looking," a beginner's class in the fine art of things to do with your eyes.

Ah, but once he got Papa there in the crosshairs, he didn't move. Didn't flinch. Just froze like a boy with a bird in the palm of his hand. Which, almost, he was.

He might still be there now, only the clock nudged us on, the clock and the notion that school had a bell that soon would be ringing.

---

strigine dance two-stepped at the delicate end of the bough. This depth-of-winter month happens to be the peak of Great Horned

But, like clockwork, each morning since, he somersaults off the end of the bed, grabs the looking lens from there on the ledge, and begins again to scan the sky, and the trees, and whoever decides to land on the roof.

He's even tried it at night. Though it's a little bit hard to make out a star with a mere binocular lens. I explained that's where the telescope comes to the rescue, but that would be the next class in the series, and we're only just fumbling with this.

I couldn't be more tickled that he's taking so deep a fancy to a sense that can take him so far, a sense that will bring more wisdom and glory than he or I or any of us, really, can ever imagine.

To see is to know, is to understand, is to absorb.

To see is to take in—from the thinnest strand of a spider's web laden with dew to the last dying ember of a star as it streaks through the cosmos—the whole of God's breath.

And it is not every day that any one of us gets a chance to instruct in using the eyes for all that they're meant to take in: The way someone fidgets a spoon while making a point at the table. The color of sky as the last beams of the day paint a pink you'll never forget. The glint of the moonlight on a pine branch heavy with snow. The gleam in the eye of someone you love.

And, oh, what of the things we can't teach, the ones we only can pray they learn on their own: How not to miss the twinge of the hurt deep in the heart; the sparkle of love blooming; the look of intent, of paying attention; how to notice a soul draining toward empty.

---

dalliance. If you put your ear to the wind, you just might hear the Great Horneds' storybook "hoo-hoo-hoooo." While owls romp,

Really, so much of it is only just seeing by feeling. It's not unlike Braille, after all. So much of the seeing that matters. It comes through the gift of the eyes, but also the touch of the skin and the skip of the heart.

But, alas, in these mornings of teaching to see, I realize I am bound, I am tethered to only the lens bobbing there on the end of the cord that slips over his head.

The rest of the teaching to see I will teach without lenses. I will teach, day after day, for as long as I'm here. I will teach my children to look and look closely.

I will teach them the glory of God is there through the lens. But they must open their hearts, as well as their eyes, to soak in the sights. To regard. To watch. To take in the world.

It is the often unnoticed to which I must teach them to pay the closest attention.

---

black bear cubs are birthed, deep in winter's cave. And the white-tailed deer bucks shed their antlers. New beginnings abound.

I Have a Dream, Too
On Envisioning

There's a grainy audiotape that loops in my head. Always does this time of year. It's the Reverend Dr. Martin Luther King Jr., launching into his "I Have a Dream" speech, from the steps of the Lincoln Memorial in Washington, D.C., back in 1963.

We have come to this hallowed spot. . . .

Every year, come the middle of January, when we pause to consider the modern-day saint and pacifist preacher, I hear the words rumbling, rise to crescendo. Goosebumps prickle down my arms and my spine.

Now is the time to rise from the dark and desolate valley. . . .

Makes me think we must all be bold—especially when it comes to dreams.

We will not be satisfied until "justice rolls down like waters and righteousness like a mighty stream."

If we don't reach deep down inside, scout around for that same bold seed, put voice to it, get up and say it out loud, put

February Field Notes: Full Snow Moon, or Hunger Moon, casts its midnight shadows on the drifts and mounds that, traditionally,

breath to it, well, then, what's the point in merely listening to someone else's dream?

I have a dream, booms the voice I hear in my head.

That dream will not leap off the couch, not without us adding to the voices. Will not rise up over the mountaintop, spill down into the valley on the other side, down to where the shadows fall—if we, too, don't dare to be so bold, to raise our hand, say, "Hmm, I, too, am dreaming."

A long, long time ago I had a real live, wide-awake dream, the sort of dream that shapes a lifetime.

My dream was in the upstairs chapel of a nunnery, far away. Out where hills rolled and corn reached toward the sky. I was only there for the weekend, for what's called a silent retreat. Which means I ate, drank, walked, and prayed in utter, total wordlessness. At least no words that you could hear. There were plenty stirring inside.

It was a Friday night, and I had eaten in silence, tucked my pj's beneath the hard slab that was serving as my bed. I tiptoed up to the chapel and there I knelt. Maybe it was all the silence, or maybe it was something else.

But as I knelt and prayed, staring at the Crucifix, staring at the long muscled legs of Jesus on the Cross, fixing on the nail holes in his palms, taking in the beautiful sorrow, and the peacefulness on his handsome Jewish face, I saw the start of what turned out to be an endless Kodak slide show of faces, one changing into another.

I saw old faces, white faces, black faces, brown faces, sallow faces, children's faces. I saw a Native American, I saw an Asian

---

*measure deepest of the year. * While Earth—at least up north—is deeply blanketed, the heavens shine at their brightest with the*

man, an old one. I saw wrinkles, I saw softness. I saw eyes and eyes and eyes. I was, of course, wiping tears from my own eyes and cheeks and chin. I can't imagine seeing such a sight and not being wholly, deeply moved. The tears, the transcendence deep inside, it's what comes when you feel, sometimes, as if a hand from heaven has just reached down and tapped you, unyieldingly, on the heart.

I knelt. I squeezed my eyes, then slowly peeked them open, to see if maybe this was all a trick that would blink away as fast as it had come. I turned, looked back, and still the faces changed.

I got the message pure and wholly: Look for—find—the face of God in everyone you meet.

The clincher to this dreamy story unfolded the next afternoon, when I returned, took a seat—near the back, I assure you—in the bigger downstairs chapel. Bravely—through spread fingers—shyly—just a little bit afraid, you might imagine—I raised my eyes again to the face of Jesus on the Cross.

At first, nothing. But then, as I softly sank into prayer, I saw a smile wash across the face of Jesus. It was all the holiness I needed—anointed confirmation, as if he whispered: "You saw just what you thought you saw."

Now you can slam the book, or flip the page right here. Or, you can read along and think, like I do, "Hmm, heaven even comes to ordinary plain-folk."

I'm no saint, but I'm now among the ones who've had a dream. Who carry it with us wherever we go from that day forth.

---

night sky's number one light: Sirius, the Dog Star, which twinkles from the shoulder of Orion's Great Dog (Canis Major). The

I carried that dream with me when I crisscrossed this country, for two months, long ago, looking for the faces—and the stories—of those who were poor, who were hungry. I carried it, day in and day out, as I poked around the city where I live and work, where, one holiday season, I collected stories of the neediest of needy folk for my newspaper. Walked into apartments way up high in dingy high-rises and narrowly made it out of one not-so-friendly two-flat where there hadn't been a speck of heat in weeks, and where someone who huddled there made it abruptly very clear that I was not welcome, not at all. I certainly carried that dream back in the days when I was a nurse, a nurse who cared for—and loved—kids with cancer, and every time I stepped to a bedside, I looked into eyes like the ones on the Cross.

I carry the dream now, in the leafy town where I live, where, ironically, it's harder to keep the dream alive because no one on the surface looks so needy, few let on to deep-down aching. Everyone is cleaned, is polished. Children carry smart phones and tablets. Play games on glowing little screens while they wait for lessons that cost, for half an hour, what some families pay for a whole week's groceries. I've learned, though, not to mistake manicured for sated, not in ways that matter.

I even hold tight to the dream—or I *try* anyway—when it tests me: When some roadster at a red light blares his horn at me, because I've dared to wait for green. When a kid down the block leaves my little one off the birthday party list—and doesn't bother trying to keep it quiet.

We all need the dream; we all need it deeply.

---

star's name means "scorcher," and its luminosity is twenty-two times greater than the sun. * Undaunted by snow—and under

Fact is, the only thing to do if we've lived a dream is to wake up every morning and tuck it in our pocket, take it where we go. Try, day after soul-grating day, to not give up, to not let down the dream. Not let the phone call go unmade, or the unkind word go uncorrected.

It is the pulse beat, really, of our every day. It is the undying belief that it is here, at our kitchen tables, in our front halls, and our workrooms, that the dream puts on its clothes. Takes on flesh and bone and matter in our every blessed hour.

The dream is in where we choose to send our children out to play. It is how we cook, and who we choose to feed. It is in the people we invite into our homes, the stories we ask them to tell, so our children can listen, can soak up sparks of wisdom that come from far beyond our walls. It is how we look into the eye of the guy pumping gas, or the pink-haired checker ringing up our groceries. And how and where we toil. It is in the getting up on Sunday morning and going out to someplace where the lessons come from far wiser teachers, instead of staying huddled round the table, flipping through the news, keeping watch of birds.

It is, day in and day out, saying to yourself: *I have a dream. I see a world other than the one before me. It starts, right now, with my next whole breath.*

---

the sparkle of big-dog star—the Great Horned Owl, amorous just last month, now settles onto her clutch of eggs; it's brood time

ORANGES-AND-CHOCOLATE BRIGADE
On Putting the Dream to Work

THE LOUDER THE ALERTS ON THE RADIO about arctic wind chills and never-before lows, the more I got to thinking about frozen people. Thinking about folks with no choice about being in the cold.

What got me thinking were the folks I was passing as I made my way through the bone-chilling day. The crews cutting down trees, their arms and legs and hands stiffly moving as they hoisted their saws in their orange puffy suits. A fellow, red-cheeked, frost-bearded, standing in the middle of the road with a pole, measuring something that couldn't wait till a day with bearable temperatures.

I thought of the mail carriers, the garbage haulers, the fire-hose aimers. I thought of the crossing guards, the meter readers, the ruptured-water-main fixers. I thought of my friend who bundles up "like an Inuit," she says, and walks twenty minutes to work, her cheeks so numb she probably can't smile when she gets there, not for a good half hour.

Then I really got to thinking about frozen people. I started

already. Tufted titmice and cardinals take their cue and join in the mating game. So too, raccoon, woodchuck, beaver, skunk,

40

thinking about Dirt Man and Tax Man and Refrigerator Man. I thought about Shorty and Squeaky and a guy named Everett, who'd built himself a multiplex of boxes up on a platform so the rats couldn't get in, down in the bowels of the city, down under Lower Wacker Drive.

I met the whole civilization of under-street inhabitants a few years ago, when I tagged along with two saints, named Frank and Kay Fennell.

Frank and Kay do an amazing, uncomplicated thing: They flip open the trunk of their car, they fill it with boxes of home-cooked food, and every Thursday night, for a good twenty years, they drive to the depths of the city.

They cruise the streets of Lower Wacker, park, stick their heads around corners, poke behind pillars. They open their trunk, spoon hot food onto plates, pour glasses of water. They feed the hungry. And this time of year, they feed the near-frozen.

When the mercury drops this low, the airwaves get crowded with news bulletins. The folks who try to make the city stumble along, they beg the homeless to come in off the streets, off the sidewalks where they stretch out on a pile of flimsy blankets, inch as close as they can to the heating vents at the bases of shimmering towers.

But the good souls who call the streets home, they aren't much interested in leaving. They've got reasons aplenty why they can't stand the shelters. And if you ask questions, if you listen, you hear the pain, you hear the fear that keeps them locked where they are.

Too often, my first instinct when arctic winds hit is to hunker

---

*and opossum. * Early bluebirds find their way, once again, to the Eastern United States. Red-winged blackbirds, one of the most*

down, to draw into my cave. But sometimes, I told myself as I thought about frozen people, you need to dig beyond that. Sometimes you need to pull up your second instinct.

And that's when I hatched what you might think is a foolish idea.

But this world needs fools almost as much as it needs something else: The courage of plain old anybodies to get up, get out of their houses, walk up to a stranger, a cold, hungry stranger, hand him or her a brown paper bag, a bag filled with oranges and chocolate. And, just as certainly, the world needs folks with the solid conviction that if we don't notice the cold hungry stranger, if we don't let him or her know that he or she isn't forgotten, we might as well pack it up, call it a day, shut out the lights, and sign off the planet.

I call it the oranges-and-chocolate brigade.

My guardian angel in these matters, Kay Fennell, once told me: "We decided it was our job to sustain [these people] for whatever their next step would be. And that might be just to stay alive for the next twenty-four hours."

So I did what Kay would do: I went to the store, got oranges and Hershey's bars, Reese's cups, too. Grabbed a stash of brown bags and started to fill. I'm headed down to the bowels of the city, where Dirt Man and Tax Man were last seen on grubby old blankets inside torn cardboard boxes, desperately trying to keep their flesh and their blood at least half alive.

Before I even get there, I'll pass the men and boys who hawk newspapers in the middle of oncoming lanes. Or one of the folks

---

abundant birds in North America, flap back home if they've wintered in warmer climes; the frontline of spring's migration.

who hovers at intersections, dodging green lights, with the signs clutched in raw, frozen fingers. "Homeless, please help."

It's not much, oranges and chocolate in a brown paper bag. But it's fuel in the cold. And it might be something a little more than that.

It might say, in case anyone's listening, that we will not let the cold and the hungry lay down one more night thinking the world has forgotten, the world has gone heartless.

That's a lot to ask of plain oranges and chocolate. But if we don't ask, who will not wake, frozen, all through?

Here's the plot, simply: Take a few lunch bags. Toss in oranges and chocolate, anything else that you fancy. Haul them to your car. You don't need to drive to the depths of the city to find cold folk. How about this: When you see someone out working, someone without much of a choice, roll down your window, stop your car. Reach out your arm, get out from behind the wheel even. Put your brown bag in his or her hand. Smile. Say what you will. Then go on your way. Or, be radical, invite that someone for a hot home-cooked dinner. Your choice. Always your choice.

FROM THE WINTER
Recipe Box

Winter's the season that draws me closest to the cook-stove. I practically purr puttering around the kitchen. All-day pots bubble away, lulling me into dreamy meditative fugues. Slow cooking, I'd wager, was made for snowy days, stay-inside days. Doughs rise. Wine-steeped stews simmer. Chowders thicken. Fruity compotes collapse into jewel-toned ooze. It's all a plethora of stove-top seduction, as what you pitch into the pot gives way, a few hours in, to heat and spice and saintly patience. It's kitchen adagio, the slow dance of surrender. And at the cookstove, trophies come dolloped on fork or soup-spoon. Either way, you won't want to dash too soon.

Beef Stew with Pomegranate Seeds, Nestled beside Aromatic Rice

The very definition of winter cookery, this aromatic number came to me from a friend who belongs among the Jazz Queens of the Kitchen. She works the stove the way Ella Fitzgerald climbed the scales, with that rare dose of confidence and cool that allows for riffing, zigging when all else might zag. You give my dear and soulful friend Susan a chord, a launching pad from which to soar—in this case, beef and pomegranate—and she takes flight. Her first rendition of the recipe read like musical notations, scribbled in the margins of the page. The barest wisps of what to do, yet grounded in seamless fluency. She knows nuance by heart, and thus can play where others toil. Cooking with Susan—or following along her kitchen notes—is pure entertainment on a long cold winter's afternoon. And the star turn at the table will bring on thunderous applause.

Provenance: This dollop of winter wonder arose from the vast imagination of kitchen wunderkind, Susan Faurot.

Prep time: 20 minutes, if beef is butcher-trimmed and you're lucky enough to find preplucked pomegranate seeds in your produce aisle (increasingly likely, as the pluses of the seeded superfruit are trumpeted round the world).

Baking time: 2 hours

Yield: 4–6 servings

   2 lb. beef chuck, cut into cubes

   2 tbsps. olive oil

   2 to 3 cloves garlic, chopped

   1 tbsp. ground cumin

   1 lb. pearl onions, skinned

2 to 4 stalks of celery, sliced thinly

5 bay leaves

Several sprigs of thyme

1 cup red wine

1 cup pomegranate juice (unsweetened)

1/3 cup chopped walnuts

1/2 cup pomegranate seeds

* Preheat oven to 300-degrees Fahrenheit.

* In a large skillet, brown the beef in 2 tbsps. olive oil; don't overcook, just brown the sides.

* Place the browned beef in a Dutch oven (or large baking dish with a lid).

* Toss with chopped garlic and cumin; add onions, celery, bay leaves, thyme. Toss again, then pour in red wine and pomegranate juice.

* Cover and place on middle rack in the oven. Bake 2 hours.

When done, remove sprigs of thyme and bay leaves. Garnish with chopped walnuts and pomegranate seeds, those garnet gems. Add chopped parsley, if you please.

Aromatic Rice

When cooking your rice (approx. 1-1/2 to 2 cups of un-cooked rice), per instructions, add the following (along, of course, with cooking water):

2-inch stick of cinnamon

2 to 3 whole cloves

2 to 3 green cardamom pods, cracked

You'll be transported to a magical someplace, far off in the Land of Deliciousness.

Spring

Season of Quickening

VERNAL (OR MARCH) EQUINOX

Nearly equal hours of light and dark occur when the tilt of Earth's axis is neither toward nor away from the sun. In fact, the sun shines squarely onto the Equator, and the planet is neatly halved with equal light, north and south. For this fleeting moment of alignment, neither side's in shadow. And the sun's crossing of the north-south divide signals the overture of the new season. In the Northern Hemisphere, the March equinox heralds spring; in the south, it brings on autumn. On either end of the globe, the "equal night" occurs around March 20.

SPRINGTIME'S WONDERLIST

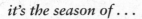

it's the season of . . .

fiddleheads, furled and heaped in balsa-wood crates, a tumult of tight-wound woodland commas . . .

unheralded—and short-breathed—warmth, carried in on southerly winds, chased off just as suddenly by insistent northerlies . . .

nest making, dialed-up by the hour, as the hatching days draw near . . .

windows shoved ajar—at last and hallelujah—because you can not stand to keep out that resurrecting vernal air . . .

crushing snowfall, and it's your heart that's crushed as the mounds flatten newly trumpeting daffodils . . .

serendipitous picnic on the lakeshore's chilly sands . . .

softening afternoons, epilogue to blanket-burrowing dawn . . .

puddles primed for rubber boots . . .

scribble your own wonders here:

A COUNT-YOUR-BLESSINGS CALENDAR:
Blessed Be Springtime, Season of Quickening

IN THE CHRISTIAN LITURGICAL CALENDAR, this is the season of Lent, leading to Eastertide, and the Paschal Mystery. In the distance, fifty days after the resurrection, stands Pentecost (literally "the fiftieth [day]"), sacred feast of Holy Spirit Infused. In the Jewish calendar, it's Passover, the Exodus from Egypt, freedom from slavery. And fifty days after the Exodus, Shavu'ot, the Jewish Festival of the First Fruits (sometimes also called Pentecost, though there's no other connection to the Christian holy day). Sacred leitmotif: Rebirth, tender beginning, resilience triumphs over winter's trial.

Here, fourteen blessings, a short-course curriculum in paying attention, slowing time, freeze-framing the essence of the quickening season, when God's world unfurls with unbridled exuberance and unparalleled pangs to the heart.

VERNAL EQUINOX: *Glory be spring, season of exodus and resurrection, of life unfurling, but, too, life tumbling from the nest. Or, sadder yet, getting pushed. It's death and life all over. To be reborn, the preachers shout, you first must die.*

BLESSING 2: *The whole top half of the world is shaking off its winter death. But death is the necessary somber note in the song of spring. Hand in hand with life. This is the season of light and shadow. And why it takes our breath away.*

BLESSING 3: *The Japanese, enlightened, teach that the beauty of the cherry blossom is its evanescence. The very fact that at any minute a breeze might blow and blossoms will be scattered. Theirs is a deep understanding of the season's essence. They're keen to what it's teaching: Behold the blossom. It won't last for long.*

BLESSING 4: *Pay attention to the barely perceptible growth of early spring. The first sprouts at the branch's far end, practically poking you in the eye, announcing, "Hey, look, I'm not just a stick anymore." Comb the earth, hike the woods. Get down on your knees, if you must. We, too, grow in barely perceptible bits. Sometimes it doesn't take much, just the barest measure of growing, of quarter-inching toward life, to make all the difference.*

BLESSING 5: *If you find a baby bird fallen from the nest to its death, whisper a proper benediction as you perform a proper burial. Lay a sprig of springtime flowers. Teach a child to do the same.*

EASTER SUNDAY: *Salute the day-after-day resurrection of the sunrise: Awake before the dawn, amble out to where you can catch the hoisting up of the fiery orb, stretch before its first-cast sunbeams, bow down, be humbled.*

BLESSING 7: *The Italians have a word* tristesse. *"Beautiful sorrow," I was told it meant. Knowing that what you love won't last. And so you love more deeply. Is this the truth of spring?*

BLESSING 8: *It's seesaw season, yin and yang. It's stripping off old skin, it's starting over. It's tender and it's green, beginning green. Everything feels tender all over. Even us, some days. Be kind to your tender spots—they just might be where essential truths seep in.*

APRIL FOOL'S DAY (APRIL 1): *Crouch down, inspect the growing things. Take note of miracles that unfold in dark of night and light of day when we're not looking, hunched inside, distracted by too-long lists of things we tell ourselves we must do. But must we, really?*

BLESSING 10: *Tiptoe outdoors once twilight deepens into darkness. Read the night sky. When you spy a twinkling star, whisper a prayer of infinite thanks for heaven's lamplights.*

MAY DAY (MAY 1): *Caretaker of Wonder Pledge: I will rescue broken flowers and ferry them to my windowsill infirmary, where I'll apply remedies and potions, or simply watch them fade away in peace.*

MOTHER'S DAY (SECOND SUNDAY IN MAY): *Tutorial in patience: Mama bird constructing her nest, one blade of grass after another. Note how she shops for just the right twig, sizing up then promptly ditching the stick that will not do. Study the ingenious troves where she gathers snips of string. We should all be so intent on our tasks.*

BLESSING 13: *Try not to be crushed in these hold-your-breath weeks when, say, your heirloom hyacinth is just beginning to bat its smoky-lavender lashes, and you wake up to find the opossums had a hoedown, broke the stalk in two. As you scoop up the remains, tuck the bloom in water, whisper a prayer, contemplate the ways you might revive your own broken dreams.*

BLESSING 14: *Bless the wildflowers, who even now, are plotting where to rise up from the summer's meadow, and who will sway beside whom. You might stroll through the nearest clearing, where first tips of green are poking through the earth, letting you in on the next season's stitch-work sampler.*

NIGHT PRAYER
On Faith, Even in the Dark

SHABBAT HAD TIPTOED IN, AS IT ALWAYS DOES, praise be to God who promised it.

Without fail, no matter what the week has washed up on our shores, Shabbat graces our table, graces the earth, as the globe is shadowed in darkness, as sunlight goes out, and candles, one by one, house by house, city by city, flicker on.

We'd lit our two candles, as always we do. We'd gobbled our fish, as the hand of the clock was sweeping toward half past the hour, and we'd not had plenty of time.

Prayers would begin any minute at the church, yes, where our synagogue dwells. The cantor would lift up a minor-key chord, the rabbi would open the book. And all of us, the few of us, gathered there would begin.

Only this Friday night I wouldn't be there.

I knew, deep in the place that knows all these things, that a room with walls and a roof, even a room with windows taller and wider than I'll ever be, wasn't big enough for my prayers.

March Field Notes: March's headline, of course, is the equinox—that biannual moment when light and dark are bisected into equal

Not this Friday night. Not at the close of this very long week when my shortlist of heartache included: a story I'd worked on for months "spiked" (newsroom lingo for left to die); our old station wagon bonked while I was out reporting a story; one no-show for Shabbat dinner, another who barely made it (after a long day's cooking, thank you), and yet another who considers fish a maternal death plot. But the tragedy that truly turned the world upside-down: a football-sized tumor found on the liver of a seventeen-year-old friend whose mother I adore, and who has already borne far too much grief.

So, while the man who I love went to pray in that room, I went to the edge of the lake. I went to where the trees reach into the night, finger the darkness. Where the dome scrapes the edge of infinity. Where no prayer is too big.

I went to the place where, uncannily, eerily, that night, the lake made no sound. Not a whimper of wave. Nothing but stillness.

Then, from out of the black, out of the dense, deep thickness that is night at the beach, I heard the lone cry of a night-flying goose. I couldn't make out its wings, couldn't see a wisp of its shadow.

All I know is I heard it, high overhead. Calling and crying and breaking the night with a sorrowful mourning song, not unlike the one in my soul.

I sat there, on the sand in the cold, looking up into the moon-less night. Not even the moon made itself known that dark night at the edge of the lake.

---

*halves, and, up north, spring slithers in (south of the Equator, autumn rushes). * Full Worm Moon, or Sap Moon, presides over*

Somewhere, though, I knew, it was out there, the moon, round and white, absorbing, reflecting, the light of the number one star. But this night it wasn't for me to see. Not this night.

Nor the chevron of geese, heading for home, riding the wind, steering straight for the polestar. Only the night-shattering cry, haunting, calling, sending chills down my bones.

And so it passed on the moonless night at the beach. Prayers spilled like waves that I couldn't hear. Floating out to the heavens that seemed to be cloaked wholly in blackness.

Fitting, I thought, as I sat there unfurling each and every petition. I couldn't see God. Couldn't hear waves. Couldn't even make out the moon.

But in none of those instances did my lack of sensation suggest absence of any kind, nor mean that nothing was there.

Just because I couldn't hear flapping of wings, didn't mean the geese were not flying.

Just because I couldn't hear luffing of waves to the shore, didn't mean the lake had gone dry.

And so with the God whose moon was lost behind clouds.

It all surrounded me, every last bit of creation. And, yes, too, Creator.

Faith is the thing that comes to you when you kneel in the dark on the sand in the night. And the lone goose calls to you, tells you it's there, up above.

Wasn't long, that dark night, till the first star crept out from the clouds. I never did see the moon.

---

the vernal do-si-do, as winter takes its exit twirl. Worm Moon, so named by Native Americans because Earth's softening (under

But, in time, I turned and headed for home. My prayers had poured out from me, filled up the night sky. Branched far and wide beyond the limbs of the tree. Skipped past the lone shining star.

I headed for home, safe in the knowing that moon and rippling water were right where they needed to be.

And, likely, God, too.

Even though all around me was darkness. Even though I couldn't see more than one step in front of me.

Prayer is like that sometimes. So is life, too.

---

extra sunlight hours) brings out earthworms, and those, in turn, beckon the red-breasted robin to return en masse. Northern

QUESTIONS WITHOUT ANSWERS
On Witnessing the Soul, Unfiltered

HANDS LOOSELY ON THE WHEEL, OLD NAVY WAGON gliding to a stop, I was blankly looking through the rain-splotched windshield when the little voice behind me shot me this:

"Mama, when we die, what will happen? Will the world start again?"

He barely gave me time to gulp, gather thought, compose an honest answer, when the rat-a-tat continued.

"Well, will I die?

"Will you?

"When will Dada die?"

I could not keep my eyes on the road. I turned and locked on his. He was looking up, looking my way, searching me for answers.

I gave him my best shot. Told him straight. Yes. Yes. And, oh, honey, we don't know.

---

tribes knew the night light as Full Crow Moon, for the cawing of crows signaled winter's end. In woodsy corners of the continent,

All three appended with this attempt at reassuring: Not for a long, long time.

Then I launched into Heaven 101, praying as I went.

How, I ask you, in the middle of a ho-hum drive to home from hockey, did the most essential questions come popping from his mouth? Why not something simple, like, Mama, can I have macaroni for my lunch?

Macaroni, I could handle. Knock that query, kazzam, clear out of the park.

Camus and Sartre, hiding under size-6 jersey, I could only fumble, hands barely groped at bat.

It is, I swear, the deepest privilege of being a mama or a papa, or a someone who breathes in sync with little people. Being the first pair of ears to hear these questions as they leap from a child's soul. To witness from front row the human mind expand, go deeper, gather goods to last a lifetime.

It is Self, unedited. It is the child's quintessential work, exploring the unknown. Making sense of everything from how the dandelion blows to what happens when he or she is no longer. Asking giant questions of the universe, and aiming them, first shot out, at the original sounding board of life.

In the case of my little boy, that would most often be me, the one who birthed him, nursed him, rocked him through his early, howling bedtime hours. As I'm still the one he's with the most hours of the day, I'm pretty much the moving target on which he throws his thinking-child darts.

---

the natives paid more attention to March as the month when sap begins to flow. Thus, woodland natives went with "Sap" as the

Out of the blue, left field, in the middle of a meatloaf, the questions come hurling. There is no agenda in a child's mind, no timetable for when a question comes. In the seamlessness of mind and soul, the question is posed in the midst of its creation.

You never have a clue, never get a notice, that your very breath might soon be sucked away by the tender beauty, the monumental power, of the unexpected puzzle of the hour.

It is, for all of us who spend the day in striking distance of a child's heart, the often-unrepeated script. The lost dialogue you can never seize again. It unspools so suddenly, so without ceremony, you can sometimes only hope that you'll remember. But then the business of the day shoves the thought aside, and no matter how you try, you can't retrieve the words, or the magic of the moment.

Sure, we sometimes hear the silly lines, over and over. Used to be, you'd find them tucked in the pages of that monthly compendium, *Reader's Digest*. Nowadays, they come in forwarded emails, alleged collections of the darnedest things that children say. I often laugh then hit delete.

But what about when the script comes tumbling forth in real time, and you're the only one who hears? You're the one who gets to fill in blanks, connect the dots, pick *a* or *b* or *c*, all of the above. Take a stab at the deepest truths known to humankind.

Because I've worked for many years in a newsroom, been a notebook-bearing gatherer of who said what and precisely how they said it, I have a rather unstoppable inclination to reach for pen whenever quotes unfurl.

---

*moniker for this month's moon. * If you saunter by the woods—*
or tarry by a pond—perk your ears and take in the high-pitched

Especially ones that nearly make me wreck the car (although you might argue that scribbling while trying to hold the wheel only enhances the chance of body shop in my offing).

Of all the wise souls I have quoted, and I have quoted many, I don't think that any lines have done as much for stealing breath as the ones I've caught while stirring, while steering, or while scrubbing curly hair.

The jottings that I jot, long ago from Thinker 1 and now from Thinker 2, are in fact a firsthand record of the unfolding of a child's soul, even when the questions are hard to hear, the answers harder to come by.

It's life unscripted that makes for Holiest Scripture.

---

vibrato of spring peepers, wood frogs, or chorus frogs who rev their croakers late in the month. This, too, is when Sandhill Cranes

PRACTICING 10
On Astonishments along the Way to Stillness

THERE IS AN ART TO BEING STILL, and I am practicing.

The birth of the day, it seems, is the hour that calls me. And, actually, all I'm going for is a mere slice of that hour. Ten minutes, for starters. For beginners like me.

There is little hope, I figure, of trying to squeeze it in, in the thick of the day, between all the rushing and dashing and typing and trolling for words.

And, at the end of the day, when the blanket of stars are out and the house is winding down to a hum, I figure my brain has gone blank, in that numb—not that crisp—sort of a way. Or, worse, it's so overstuffed by that hour that all I'd do is churn and rechurn whatever the day had left in its wake. There'd be no stillness within.

It's hard enough at the dawn. Hard enough to keep the tick-tock at bay.

---

migrate north. And it's the peak of waterfowl migration, when Tundra Swans and loons and Blue-winged Teals are passing ink

But I've begun.

Before the first dabs of light are soaking the low-down sky, I am tiptoeing out of my bed, stumbling downstairs, scooping my coffee beans. The cat, always hungry, demands his share of my morning attentions—and his own scoop from the tin in the fridge.

Then, warm mug cupped in my palms, I reach for the door and step under the holiest dome, the dome of the dawn as it breaks into double-time spring.

And that's when it hit me, my first morning out: I'd just stepped into a cauldron of birdsong soup. There were so many layers of so many sounds, coming from so many places, my ears— at first—could barely pick it apart.

There were trills and caw-caws and whistles and chatter. Short notes and fat notes. And notes that seemed without end, twisting and tumbling and climbing again. Notes most insistent, and notes that dribbled off, into ellipses.

And it all, all at once, seemed to be moving, whirling around me, as one song took flight, and soared to a nearby limb. Or criss-crossed the sky. Or merely hopped down the branch, in search of a cozier, noisier perch.

It was surround sound at its most heavenly, this ever-circling orchestral creation, powered by wings and lungs whose weights would be measured in grams. A whole-bodied chorister not even one ounce.

And all I knew that very first morning was that everywhere I listened, there was a full-throttle soundtrack not to be missed.

---

dabs in the sky. * Mourning Doves take to nesting now. Gold-finches molt into their brilliant saffron robes. The morning song of

One I'd too often slept through. Or, sadder, ignored in my packing of lunches and checking of schedules.

It wasn't as if this was new, this Spanish moss of birdsong, dripping from trees.

It's been there, just beyond the panes of the windows, the other side of the door.

It was only that I'd not carved out the wisp of an hour, made room for the stillness, so that what was there all along could make its way into my eardrums and down to my soul.

Once my head stopped spinning, I did what any student of stillness must do: I planted myself firmly, solidly, on the seat of the bench in my not-so-secret garden, the one that runs along the kitchen, the one that meanders, the one that catches the morning's first light.

And I started to look, not to glance but to study.

It wasn't hard.

I sat and watched chives grow, those early-spring straight-backed soldiers of pungence, the ones I'm already snipping, not unlike bits of newly-mown grass that I bring in for breakfast.

I have to admit, stillness didn't come easy. Wasn't a natural fit, not for me, anyway.

Before my ten minutes was clocked, I was itching to dig in the dirt. I'd tallied a list that beckoned me and my ministrations: the climbing hydrangea that needed a lifeguard, weeds that might do with a shrill short blast of a whistle, demanding they stop in their trespassing tracks.

---

cardinal, finch, and dove is so insistent, sleepyheads have been known to rise to slam the bedroom windows. Woodpeckers stake

But I also noticed this: The longer you sit in rapt silence, utter attention, the deeper you sink into the whole of it, the line between you and the earth and the sky and the dew all but evaporating.

My next morning out, it was chilly. And a soft morning's rain added its backbeat to the birdsong. So I sat with my stillness on an old wicker chair, inside the porch with the screens. From across the garden and under the pines, I listened to raindrops measuring time with the ping-ping-ping from the downspouts.

While it's not yet under my skin, this time-out for the soul, I can feel it working its way to the wellspring, this sacred act of tiptoeing out of bed to catch the morning unaware.

And in the calm of the dawn, I might remember the words to the prayer that, for too long, have been dimmed. And very much missing.

---

*their turf with rat-a-tat drill to old dead wood. * Beware the skunk, out trolling for a perfumed mate. * The night sky of early spring*

EMERGENCY BLANKET
On Holy Pauses and Joy-Taking

IT DWELLS, AS TOO MANY THINGS DO, in the back of my old blue station wagon, the car so old it predates the cupholder as standard feature.

It once was a wedding present from a friend I dearly love. For years and years it covered our bed. Then the bed of the boys who came two and ten years after the wedding. But, eventually, it started getting so holey I feared it might wend its way around my little one's neck some night, so off the bed it came.

In the back of the car it landed.

Which, it turns out, is a most essential thing.

The blanket, now, has a much more important job than keeping arms and legs and little pink toes covered through the night.

The blanket, now, is in charge of instant, spontaneous, *and* unanticipated taking time out. The blanket, indeed, is for emergencies.

Emergency blanket, that's what the safety guides call it; scold us to keep one in case of emergency. Just so happens that in my old wagon—though screeching brakes *are* often involved—the

belongs to Cancer, the crab. Ancient cultures believed Cancer
to have been the gate through which souls passed, from heaven

emergency is not so much tumbling into the ditch or running out of gas in the middle of nowhere. More like sating the urge to suddenly and without notice fling yourself to the ground, glance skyward, for cloud watch or picnic.

A sad thing about me—or one of them, at least—is that I am not a natural-born disciple of the time-out. That's a subject in which I've always needed extra schooling.

I remember long ago being home from college on spring break and being holed in my room for, oh, ten hours straight, memorizing every last function in the human body for a whopper of a physiology exam. I remember my papa, a man known to keep *his* fingers to the keyboard for sessions that routinely went late into the night, coming to my room, practically nabbing me by the neck, offering forth one of his famous Papa-isms: "The wise man says, 'He who keeps his nose to the grindstone gets nothing but a sharp nose.' "

And so he ushered me out the door, down the stairs, and off to some silly movie.

I still need prompts. I still need Post-its stuck around my life, reminding me that not every hour need be for getting something done.

I still need, basically, someone to grab me by the neck, point me down the stairs, turn me in the direction of silly movies.

My papa's not around, so I keep my blanket near at hand. In fact, I travel—twelve months a year—with my holey blanket.

Proof of its indispensability tumbled undeniably forth one glorious spring day in the thick of spring break, when the old wagon, my two boys, and I turned in at the lighthouse parking lot instead of driving by. During spring break, the little town where

---

toward Earth, as they slid into human bodies at birth. The most famous bright lights of Cancer are known as "the beehive cluster."

we live all but empties, as flocks flee south for radiant beaches and undiluted sun. But we, odd ducks, stick close to home and our chilly beaches along Lake Michigan, less than a five-minute drive from where our blanket resides.

I lurched the car into park, slung backpack over shoulders, and, while wondering eyes absorbed the shock, I hauled that blanket from the back.

"C'mon boys," I shouted over my shoulder, headed down the hill. "We're going to the beach."

My whole point in dwelling on the ratty old blanket, of course, is that it's stitched with a particular wisdom: The most essential grace of stopping time sometimes. Hitting the proverbial pause. Even if, especially if, you're not a million miles from home, and you've not packed a suitcase.

The Zen Buddhists teach us well, and Muslims too: Take time out of your day. Carve deep places for quiet contemplation. And don't forget the prayer of the unplanned picnic.

To gather on a beach, to bury legs in sand. To watch the waters ebb and flow. It can be a holy moment. The sacred sound of laughing with your children, or anyone you love.

There is unending grace, it seems, in allowing an ordinary moment to turn itself inside out, to expose the whimsy of an hour when all that really matters is that you're not doing the thing you thought you would have been, should have been.

So here's the prompt: Be ready in an instant. Don't leave home without your holey blanket.

The Greco-Roman astronomer Ptolemy called it "the nebulous mass in the breast of Cancer," and it was one of the first heavenly masses Galileo pinned under his telescope.

HOURS OF DAPPLED SHADOW
On Sacred Invitation

W E SAT STRETCHED OUT IN THE WINDOW, my firstborn and I, our stockinged feet just barely touching.

We sat stretched out in the window in the hours of darkness on the afternoon of the day we call Good Friday. But really it is Shadowed Friday. Friday of dappled afternoon, dark and light, as sunbeams played on the pages of words he allowed me to read aloud.

I invited my Jewish-souled child into my room, where always on this very deep Friday, I grow quiet, honor the story with my silence and prayer. Insist, in a very old-fashioned way, that the whole house be shrouded, be deep, be filled with silent prayer.

I've never been one to push what I believe. Rather I offer it out, a wisp, a seed, at a time. Gauge the winds, see if it catches.

This Friday, though, as the hand of the clock swept past twelve, ticked toward three, the hours when the nuns and my mother

April Field Notes: Poetically, Full Pink Moon glows down on the first flowering of the carpet herb "moss pink," another name

taught me to keep watch on the skies, to watch the darkness roll in, eclipse the sun, remember the sorrow, I started to read.

What I read were words from Caryll Houselander, a twentieth-century British Catholic mystic sometimes called "that Divine Eccentric," what with her chain-smoking tendencies and procliv-ity for profanity (to say nothing of her dalliance with the master spy who served as the model for Ian Fleming's James Bond).

Tucked in the years-yellowed pages of the Bible that dates from my Jesuit college days, I'd found the stapled-together pages of "The Way of the Cross," my church's adaptation of the prayers from Houselander's 1955 meditative journey through Jesus' Passion, the trail of so many tears from the moment Jesus is condemned to his death, to his Crucifixion, to the laying of his body into the tomb.

I got no deeper in than the First Station, the condemning of Jesus, when I inhaled the imploring, "Lord, that I may see!"

And then, deeper still, I read the plea: "Let me recognize You, not only in saints and martyrs, in the innocence of children, in the patience of old people waiting quietly for death, in the splendor of those who die for others; but let me also discern Your beauty through the ugliness of suffering. . . . Let us know You in those who are outcast, humiliated, ridiculed, shamed; in the sinner who weeps for sins committed."

It was then, after reading those words, alone and suddenly achingly lonely, that I realized I wanted to invite him, my first-born, into my chamber of prayer.

It was then, realizing the whole of my life view was held up in these stanzas and lines—the notion that the Divine dwells within

for wild ground phlox, one of springtime's head-start wild-flowers. The luminous orb on high is also known as Sprouting

every last one of us, if only we take the time and heart to see, truly to see—that I thought I might cast one of my seeds, see if it caught, if it mattered.

For the past two nights, the start of the eight-day Jewish feast of Passover, which often falls in Passion Week, we'd told and retold the Exodus story, how the Israelites escaped the slavery of Egypt and Pharaoh, how Moses lifted a rod and parted the Red Sea. I'd listened, asked questions, paid attention when one wise friend at the Seder table spoke of the power of myth. How verifiable fact isn't the point, but Truth is.

And how myth in the end is all about Truth, all about passing on kernels and seeds and endosperm truths. And praying that somehow, maybe, it takes, sends out its own tender shoot.

I thought, as my wise friend spoke, of my own dappled years, years of shadow and light, of doubt and belief, of knowing and not.

I thought as I read through the words, the Way of the Cross, as I was warmed in the light of the sun pouring in, soft against the pillows and blankets, that these words truly feed me.

And that's when I thought: Let me give him a taste, my child who once had asked who tucked in God at the end of the day, when it was time for sleep to come to all who'd toiled all day.

That's when I called to him, invited him in. Can I read you the Stations, I asked? Can I read you the Way of the Cross, unspooled in modern-day terms?

"Oh, sure, I'd love that," he answered quite quickly.

I admit to a skip in my heart.

And then we sat, he and I, warm under blankets, our toes just

---

Grass Moon, Egg Moon, or Fish Moon, as, back when Native Americans were putting names to shining moon, April was

barely touching, as page after page, I read this modern and moving interpretation of the Way of the Cross.

We considered how Jesus fell three times under the weight of the cross-thatched timbers, considered him stopping to talk to the women along the side of the road, considered Veronica wiping his face, read these words from the Sixth Station's text:

"Drive me by the strength of your tenderness to come close to human pain . . . . Give me Your hands to tend to the wounds of the body and the wounds of the mind. Give me Your eyes to discern the beauty of your face, hidden under the world's sorrow. Give me the grace to be a Veronica; to wipe away the ugliness of sin from the human face."

My firstborn listened as I read, and then, when I started to cry, reading the words of Jesus's third fall, considering all the falls of my own, the stumblings, he looked up quietly, compassionately, touching my face with his gaze.

He sighed as I sighed.

And then, after I'd read of the dying on the Cross, and the laying in the tomb, we both sat in the dappled light, the shadows crossing the sky, the sky ever-so-faintly turning to gray.

He fell asleep, my firstborn.

And I lay there, praying and wondering, wondering and praying.

That is how I spent the hours of dappled shadow, the hours of knowing that in light and in darkness I'd found a truth and scattered the seed.

And maybe, just maybe, it took.

---

*when the rivers swelled with shimmering schools, and shad, especially, swam upstream to spawn. * Southerly winds — and*

INTO THE WOODS
On Exulting

Leave it to the Italians. They have a name for Easter Monday. They call it *Pasquetta*, or "Little Easter."

Why, they wonder, after all the deprivation and darkness of Lent, the shadow that burst, finally, into light, into the unbridled exuberance of Easter, why pack it up like so many leftover baskets, and tuck it on the shelf till next year?

Those smart Italians, they do a very smart thing: They grab one of those baskets, they pack it with leftover deliciousness from Easter, and they take to the woods. Specifically, they set out in search of a watery place.

Water, on *Pasquetta*, is key. There is, depending on your level of dedication—and moisture tolerance—some splashing involved.

In fact, all over Europe on the day after Easter, there are folks splashing. They are partaking of the Little Easter blessing.

In Hungary, apparently, boys knock on doors. Girls answer.

---

the shift in sunlight's angle—rustle songbirds from their sun-drenched winter outposts, and dispatch them onto migration's

Boys splash girls. Girls invite them inside. They feast. They send boys home with wildly painted Easter eggs.

On Easter Tuesday, the girls return the favor. They knock and splash.

It must be riotous, all this knocking and splashing and heading to the woods with your leftover pink and green eggs.

But, besides the fact that it's quaint, there is, it seems, something rich about the European approach to Little Easter. To all of life, perhaps, but certainly to Little Easter.

It is about taking linear measure of time, peeling back the ordinary, extracting mystery and sacred, raising simple hours into the realm of the extraordinary. It is about pushing away the rock of workday expectation, exploring the cavern of the deep unknown, the unexpected. Reveling on a Monday.

Because a friend I love had been telling me for months I needed to, had to, must not sleep until I read *To Dance with God*, a poetic, eye-opening 245 pages on family ritual and community celebration written by Gertrud Mueller Nelson, I'd finally cracked the cover.

My friend was right. Gertrude Mueller Nelson is deeply Jungian, deeply spiritual, and very wise. She says this of what she calls "holy time out":

"Holes are created in time through the creation of holidays—or, indeed, holy days—where the ordinary and everyday stops and time is set apart and not *used*. Every seventh day (sabbatical) since the story of creation is a day of being, a 'day of rest.' That is what a feast is. The feast has its origin and its

---

north-bound flyway. Nesting season, for most winged flocks, is at its peak. Canadian geese, ahead of the pack, start hatching.

justification in its dedication to celebrating and worship. It belongs to the gods."

She goes on to tell us that Plato, of all thinkers, put it this way: "The gods, taking pity on mankind, born to work, laid down a succession of recurring feasts, to restore them from fatigue and gave them the Muses and Apollo, their leader, and Dionysis, as *companions* in their feasts—so that, nourishing themselves in festive companionship with the gods, they should again stand upright and erect."

The feast—or holy day—then, Nelson writes, is "the very act which makes the transition from crawling beasts to the upright and conscious human, a transformation which makes what is human equal to and a companion (comrade) of the gods."

Hmm. At our house, come to think of it, we don't spend a whole lot of time noticing feast days, let alone packing our baskets and heading to the woods.

Apparently, Gertrud does. She says that on Easter Monday she always let her children stay home from school. They went off to church early in the morning, but then they took to the woods, often to a marshy place. Through binoculars, they watched the water birds, the mating birds, engaged in their vernal entwinements. They inhaled the woods, the little tips of tender green budding on all the branches, turning the gray of winter woods into the lacy green of early spring.

Getting wet, she says, was always part of the picnic. Back to the baptismal waters, and the holy sprinklings, that are so very much a part of Easter.

---

* *Dragonflies, those mysterious bi-wings, take to the air. Pond turtles arise from the depths, basking in the warming sun.*

Immediately, I found all of this a notion I could warm to: an excuse for a picnic. Tromping through the woods. Stopping time for one more day. Stealing children from the classroom, for the sake of exuberating spring, to concoct a verb.

That night, well past sleeping time, I tiptoed in the dark to the bedside of my firstborn, the one who loves the woods and who also had just flicked out the light when he heard me coming up the stairs. I told him my Little Easter idea. At first, he broke into a grin (he turned the light back on, that's how I know that), but then he thought about the school day, and decided, not even for a lunch-hour picnic, could he leave the load at hand.

Oh, well, I sighed. Fact is, we seemed to have done our Little Easter backwards. We had taken to the woods already, on big Easter. Taken Kosher-for-Passover-for-Easter picnic to the woods, in our glorious whirling of religions. It seemed the place to be, the woods that is. For all the reasons above.

But still, I think, I might take my little one, the one without such a school load, on a *Pasquetta* picnic. Or maybe, in the twilight, I'll take both my boys by the hand, take them off to where the gods urge us to recline. Just one more day, a holy day.

A holy day for splashing in the woods. I like this Little Easter.

---

*American toads commence their tripped-alarm trill. * Flowering trees—redbud, serviceberry, dogwood, to name but a few—froth*

OF LILACS AND PILLOWCASES AND SLOW LAST BREATHS
On Grace at the Hour of Death

THE PHONE RANG. THROUGH BROKEN WORDS I made out this: "My mom's gonna die. In the next few days."

It was my friend Susan. It was my friend who had always counted her mother as pretty much her dearest, best-loved friend. It was my friend who, for months, and especially in the last few weeks, had been inching ever closer to the inconceivable conclusion that I just heard her put to words—sputter, choke through, really—on the other end of the line.

Her blessed, tiny mother—the one who, one week away from turning seventy-nine, still sold houses, still filled her calendar with lunches and theater and friends upon friends before the cancer, damn cancer, truly demanded center stage—her mother was, at last, unavoidably, in her final holy hours.

She'd been moved just the night before into intensive care to try to ease her gasping broken breathing. And she was now, they

---

at the bough. Deep in the woods, deer sprout antlers. And morel mushrooms, too, partake of sprouting's overdrive, deep in the

had just decided, being moved out. Moved out, said Susan, to a room where she would die. Untethered. Except for the slow drip of morphine, liquid mercy doled out in fractions of a milliliter.

"She's too brittle to move home," said Susan, who wished for that more than anything.

So did her mother.

"I just want to go home and drink a cold glass of water," her mother had said, the day before, one of the few lucid sentences she spoke on that day when she couldn't, for the life of her, catch her breath.

Susan, who had stayed dry-eyed and unwobbly through most of this long road, was without words. I heard tears falling. "It'll be okay. I'll close the door. It'll be quiet," she whispered.

I suddenly saw lilacs.

Get lilacs. Fill the room. I said the words softly. The words came from my mouth, but really they came from somewhere else. I kept going. Make it smell like heaven. Get her pillow, a soft pillow. Play music. Hearing is the last earthly thread to go.

Light a candle. No, strike that. Oxygen and candles aren't a good idea. Combustion of this sort, you do not need. Susan laughed. Softly. She had room, bless her, in her heart for laughing.

Make a soft nest.

I thought of the womb that carries us into life, the gentle soothing waters. The lub-dub of a mother's heart. The way it must pound in all-enveloping waves through the almighty contraction that pulses one life through and out of another.

I thought of death. I thought of how I would want to be

Midwest woodlands especially. All the world's bristling in these return-to-glory hours.

ushered out in the same soft womb of soothing waters. Fill my room with springtime rushing in. Lay my cheek on smooth white cotton, French knots and tiny forget-me-nots hand-stitched along the pillowcase's edge. Anoint me with lavender waters. Put cold water to my lips. And make it sweet, while you're at it.

If, that is, we are so blessed to know that we are headed heaven's way. If we have a little notice. Say, an hour or a day.

Susan whispered yes. Yes, to hyacinth. Yes, to going to her mother's bed, her real one, not the one that's making do in the ICU, and gathering the pillow that knew the contours of her mother's cheeks and chin and forehead, the contours, too, of all her mother's dreams.

Since I was already speaking from a place that doesn't often see the light, I kept on going. There are times in life when all is scraped away, and there is time and room only for the essence. This was such a time.

"Susan, death is beautiful. I don't know if you've ever been right there when someone dies. But it will fill you with unimaginable peace. Something rushes into the room. You are not afraid. You know that you are not alone. There is something full of grace that holds you."

Susan whispered yes.

And I went off to fill my arms with lilac and hyacinth and the sacred earthly incense that would carry my dear friend's most blessed mother on her way to heaven.

KNIT 1, PRAY 2
On Wrapping Each Other in Believing

THE WOMEN CAME THE WAY WOMEN OFTEN COME, filing in in dribs and drabs, once they'd wrapped up the business of their day. Obligations out of the way, time now to get down to why we're really on this planet.

There was among us, one in need. Very much so. And we were there, armed with slender wooden sticks and balls of yarn soft as kitten's fur. And prayer. Skeins of prayer.

These women call themselves "The Shawl Sisters," and their task was to knit a prayer shawl for a child, a girl of seventeen, who was headed off to a faraway city where she'd meet up with a phalanx of oncologists, cancer doctors, who would peer into her liver and prognosticate the days—and, God willing, years—ahead.

She would be wrapped, this girl too young for what had taken hostage her liver, in soft looped stitches. Some too tight, some too loose. Some missing altogether. But each one noosed and pulled with prayer.

May Field Notes: In this month of memory, Full Flower Moon, or Corn Planting Moon (Algonquin) or Milk Moon (an old-time

As she lay on hard cold tables, as she leaned against stiff, rough hospital sheets, ones washed ten thousand times, she would be cloaked, this child, in the tender labor of tired women who'd do anything to soften the hard blows. Insulate the chill. Take away the hurt.

The equation was simple, and ancient: Women gathered, as they've done since there were threads to be pulled through cloth, strands to be woven into squares, crocheted into circles, the geometries of home life so elemental and everywhere.

Cradling sewing baskets and knitting bags, drawn into circles on dusty prairies or candle-lit cabins—or the well-upholstered dining room in a leafy, tranquil town—women have come to tend the stitches of one another's lives, to patch together what it is that aims to leave us tattered. Or in pieces on the floor.

As the night wore on, as teacups were filled, the cake plate passed, time and tempo were measured in murmured words and click-click-click of wooden needles, slipping through the loops of yarn.

We knit 1, prayed 2. And in between we purled across the rows of our life: the prom dates and all their dramas. The stormy weather just ahead. The recipe for chicken salad.

Then at last, late from a meeting, dressed in pointy-toed heels, flush from rushing up the highway, the one among us arrived, the mama of the one for whom the knitting started three short months ago.

She came with news: Not only need we pray for her second born, the one who'd soon be wrapped in the shawl, but also her

nod to bovine abundance, when cows could be milked three times a day), pours creamily across field and brook, peak and

fourth born, who'd just come home from the hospital himself. He'd been running a fever for six nights and six days.

Her fourth born, you see, has leukemia, and a spiking fever is never good.

This mama bears more than any shawl could hold—or so you'd think. Until you heard her laugh. Until you heard her swear with all her heart that all would be well, dammit.

It had to be.

And then she told us, worst of all, as if all that was preamble, that the deepest need for prayer this night was this: a call that had come at five o'clock that morning. A suicide; a cousin, long plagued, had leapt off a bridge. Her beloved aunt, she insisted, was the one who needed prayer; not she, the mother of two children bearing cancer.

And so the women dropped their needles, clasped hands, and prayed.

It went that way for hours, the seamless intermingling of the prosaic and the prayerful. And so, too, the laughter flowing into tears.

There is much to pray for, always. But especially so this night, where the women came with petitions and pieces of a prayer shawl.

It is apt, I realized, that women so often turn to spools of thread, and rolled-up balls of yarn when life seems to be unraveling at the edges. When it seems the strands that hold us together are being tugged at, torn, mercilessly.

"We're knitting toward the mystery," said the woman sitting

---

*valley. All the world's abloom in May, and thus the lunar label. Virgo, the maiden, sparkles in the night sky. * Closer to Earth,* next to me, a beautiful woman with bare, muscled arms. "The prayerfulness of knitting is a long tradition."

One by one, stories were told of how knitting had been the occupation of choice at the side of so many deathbeds.

One woman told how when her husband lay dying he was wrapped first in a Jewish prayer shawl, and his tumors went away. And then, months later, she was handed a knitted shawl, knitted by Catholic women who'd thought to knit in prayer medallions, and ones of patron saints, and how in desperation she'd flung it round her dying husband's shoulders. She believed, she said, in the power of a prayer shawl. And you knew she meant it.

Someone else mentioned that when you are furiously knitting, you need pay some attention, and thus your mind is blocked from thinking all the other things that haunt you in a room where someone's dying.

But this night, it was all about believing.

Why, the yarn was even green, the color of a meadow in the spring, when it's shaking off the drab of winter, bursting feverishly into life. The earthiest of greens.

And this night, the prayer with every stitch was that the cancer would be nowhere found. Vanquished. Sent to hell to stay there. The only place where it belonged.

Fervently, the mama of the shawl child worked those needles. Click-click-clicking all the while.

At last, two pieces were complete. No rows, it seemed, were much the same. It was plenty holey here and there. But it was beautiful, all right, the handiwork of many hands and hearts.

---

all's at full tilt. The bird world's atwitter with what amounts to courtship, and, certain of the outcome, nests are feathered with

Time to join the ends, the mama declared. Her sweet girl's shawl was nearly ready. All talking lulled while she put her mind to this knitting task—how to make it whole.

And then one knitter in the circle—a doctor—one who'd come with crochet hooks, just in case, pulled them from her bag, held them poised. Dove in, as if the surgeon.

More clicking followed. Breaths were held all around.

And then she held up the shawl, case closed. And the mama flung it round her shoulders. Beamed. She's a believer, this mama.

And she is sure as sure can be that what they'd done, those nights as winter turned to spring and they'd clicked and prayed, and prayed and clicked, was knit their way to holy resurrection.

a vengeance. Cedar Waxwings, among the love birds, pass
berries or flower petals back and forth, beak to beak, avian

POWER CORD
On Prayerful Attention

WEEK AFTER WEEK, I REMIND MYSELF THAT, come Friday, I ought to set my alarm a good hour earlier than all the rest of the days, even though it's the one day I needn't get up to go to work. Rather, it's so I can slip out from under the sheets and cloak myself in the velvet hours of night giving way to dawn.

So I could slither into my garden, curl up on the creaky bench, not unlike an inchworm in repose, and spy on all the doings of the morn.

I could, perhaps, watch the shrunken globes of dew catch first light, cast a hundred itty-bitty rainbows, a daily morning magic show for those who, like the robin and the cardinal, do not waste the dawn in slumber.

I could, if I was lucky, catch the fronds of fern unfurling, as the fiddleheads let loose their clenched-fist grip, give way to warming rays, awaken to the sun.

---

affection at its swooningest. Red Knots, those hungry shore-birds, gorge on horseshoe-crab eggs in the Delaware Bay.

I might catch the first flash of golden yellow feathers, papa goldfinch, pecking at the thistle seed.

I might even be there to greet the hungry cat as he moseys back from all his midnight mischief, staggering round the garden bend, stopping for a slurpy drink from the mossy bowl where robins splash and preen.

No wonder Friday morning's hours are the ones I call religion.

Yes, I need to pack lunches, chase children out the door. There are chores aplenty all day long. But it's the one day I set aside for meditation, prayers that needn't be Spanxed into too-tight slots.

I might catch a snatch of blessed-be's here or there on my downtown working days, gazing out the windows of the train as it rolls past a cemetery, rumbling through the city. Or peering down an alley, watching a teetering old man picking through the garbage. I find time to stitch deep thoughts throughout my week. But I don't have unbroken time too often.

And that's why I call Friday mornings my three-pronged power cord.

I plug my soul back into the One who puts the Holy into what's on high, and what's beneath our feet. More than almost anywhere, I hear the whispers of the Divine when I am crouched down low to Earth in all her glory.

When I am wrapped in birdsong. When the saintly soprano of the wren sends shivers down my spine. When I am close enough to holiness itself to hear the rush of the blue jay's wing as she flutters by.

Warbler migration—more than one thousand miles in a single stretch, most often atop night winds, pulled in droves as if by

When I am filling my lungs with the incense that wafts from my Korean spice viburnum, a sacrament on branches if ever there was one.

It is these earthly tendrils—the touch, the sound, the smell—that spool me in, bring me back to the simple, undeniable truth that all of us, inhabitants of sky and soul and garden, are infused with breath from one sole source.

And it awakens me, pulls me to attention, more than all the clatter in a world that stands to lose the art of listening.

It's some cathedral, the place in which I cast my morning prayer. And it's the breeze rushing off the lake that carries me to where I meet the heart, the hand of God.

---

*magnet—comes so thick, verily a cloud—albeit one that warbles when it takes to trees. And wastes little time before multiplying the species. * Monarch butterflies lay eggs, but only on milkweed, and preferably on its leafy undersides. White-tailed deer birth fawns. Striped skunk litters, and snapping turtles, come out from hiding. * In the waning days of May, hummingbirds astound, migrating through the Great Lakes flyway at a clip of roughly twenty miles per day, a Herculean feat for a creature that weighs no more than five extra-strength aspirin, and flaps its itty-bitty wings eighty times per second, or nearly seven million flaps a day.*

FROM THE SPRINGTIME
Recipe Box

Certainly, it's the farmer's field—asparagus bed, in
particular—that captures the vernal imagination—and
mine. But in my growing-up days, spring meant Easter
holiday, which meant a six-hour road trip, Chicago to
Cincinnati, and my grandma's ivy-covered house on the
hill. Once our old wood-paneled station wagon pulled
to a stop at the bottom of the scary-steep driveway just
outside the butter-bathed kitchen, we couldn't escape the
wagon's confines quickly enough. We'd be in my grandma's ample arms, then slither past—swift as politely
possible—headed straight to the tin of Easter cut-outs
tucked belly-to-belly against the toaster. Springtime to
me will forever play the soundtrack of lifting the lid on
a menagerie of chicks and bunnies, ducklings and lambs,
and golden-edged eggs, all nesting atop crinkly wax-
paper beds.

Oma Lucille's Famous
Rolled Cut-Out Cookies

There was always a tin on the yellow pre-Formica counter.
She had a habit of cutting flowers, mostly roses, from the
pages of slick magazines. Precision cut. Glued, taped, somehow attached to the lid of the tin. Gilding the lily, really,

because what was inside, in waxy blankets, was the taste of walking into Grandma's, and the sweet-baked perfume that, still, takes me back to North Cliff Lane, the street where my German Oma lived for half a century. As I look closely at the recipe card, I see a note that says this came from the kitchen of Elizabeth G., my grandpa's sister, Aunt Lily, yet another sturdy German baker, this one a fräulein. Spinster sister, Aunt Lily was. Ah, but she begat these, and they live on, ever, they do . . .

Provenance: Great-Aunt Lily, Elizabeth Glaser

Yield: Never enough

  1 cup shortening

  ½ cup brown sugar

  ½ cup white sugar

  1 egg

  2 tbsps. lemon juice, and grated rind

  2 cups flour

  ¼ tsp. baking soda

  ¼ tsp. salt

  Raisins, pressed into service as various body parts

* Cream shortening. Add sugar. Cream well, adding egg, flour, soda, salt, and, finally, lemon juice and rind.

* Chill about 3 hours (or overnight).

* Roll to ¼ -inch thickness.

* Deploy cookie cutters. (Baker's note: As the season demands, bunnies, chicks, ducklings, lambs, Easter eggs in spring; pumpkins, turkeys, Santa a la sleigh, as their occasions arise.)

* Plunk raisins where needed—bunny's nose, chick's beak, or, in time, Mr. Turkey's eye.

* Bake at 350-degrees Fahrenheit, 10 to 12 minutes, or until golden-rimmed.

* Let cool, then slide off cooling racks and settle on wax-paper nests.

Summer

Season of Plenitude

SUMMER (OR JUNE) SOLSTICE

The sun travels its longest arc across the northern sky, nearest the North Pole, and thus, daylight is at its longest north of the Equator. The moment the sun crosses its northernmost apex, the seasonal odometer clicks over, turning to summer in the north, and to winter south of the Equator. The closer you come to the globe's tip-top axis, the more abundantly you find yourself in the Land of the Midnight Sun. And the light-filled benchmark falls on or around June 21.

SUMMERTIME'S WONDERLIST

—⊶∞⊷—

it's the season of . . .

firefly flicker: the original flash of wonder . . .

fledgling's first flight, lesson in resilience . . .

cricket chorus, that chirpity blanket tucking in the nighttime, "audible stillness" in the poetry of nathaniel hawthorne . . .

butterfly couplet shimmering across the lazy afternoon . . .

sweet corn, buttered, dripping down your chin . . .

ditto: the peach . . .

putting thumb to the hose: water therapy at its most meditative . . .

Perseid's meteoric chalk marks etched across the blackboard of midsummer's predawn sky . . .

scribble your own here:

A COUNT-YOUR-BLESSINGS CALENDAR:
Blessed Be Summer,
Season of Plenitude

IN THE CHRISTIAN LITURGICAL CALENDAR, this is Ordinary Time, the summer's lull between Pentecost and Advent, far off. In the Hebrew calendar—one with deep agrarian roots—this, too, is quiet time for holy days and festivals. The bounty is in the farmer's fields, and hands are deep in the faith-filled acts of tilling, hauling water buckets, praying for rains, but not too much, weeding, and daily gleanings. It is in this ordinary time, one filled with quotidian mystery and miracle, that the extraordinary waits to be unearthed.

Here, fourteen blessings, meditative Post-its to remind us that we abound in holiness.

SUMMER SOLSTICE: *Celebrate the longest day to bask in sunbeams. Play shadow games. Count your freckles. Scatter sunflower seeds to the wind. Watch them grow, turn their heads to the sun as if to nod their thank you. From sunup to sundown, frolic. Marvel at all that mighty sun can do for little us.*

MIDSUMMER'S DAY (JUNE 24): *Praised be the prodigal light that ever rises and sets. Hidden through the night, it returns, peeking over the straight-edged distance, every dawn. That we might absorb the faithfulness and come to know: The light will always come.*

BLESSING 3: *Some consider it religion to grow a garden. Like any act of faith, it sometimes shatters hearts. But, more often, takes your breath away.*

INDEPENDENCE DAY (JULY 4): *Awaiting nighttime's fireworks: Is it not the darnedest thing that, when sitting at the drawing board, God thought to make a bug with taillights? Call it firefly or lightning bug or blinking-bellied beetle. Mostly, it's a gentle nudge if you're out in darkness: Burst of light will come. Promise blinking in the distance. Hope is here, the taillight tells you, even when you cannot see it. And then, the flash.*

BLESSING 5: *Make daily rounds of the growing things in the so-called garden. Carry clippers. Cut a new bouquet every day. Tuck them in odd places, like next to children's beds, just to see if anyone notices. Whisper vespers for the lovelies.*

BLESSING 6: *"But there is still one more thing I have to do," said Miss Rumphius, of the eponymous children's picture book by Barbara Cooney, a story worth committing to heart. "I have to do something to make the world more beautiful." And so she set out to scatter lupine seeds. "All that summer Miss Rumphius, her pockets full of seeds, wandered over fields and headlands, sowing lupines." What will you sow upon this holy Earth?*

BLESSING 7: *Praised be this season of high permeability, when the outside comes rushing in, in great gulping doses through wide-open windows. And the inside, too, stirs to life, especially in nighttime, in the dappled dark, with but a moon, or flickering street lamp, draping your bedclothes in filigree shadows.*

BLESSING 8: *Praised be, too, the summer's night sounds gurgling in. The 10:04 train whistling by. Horns and siren, reminding that all is not still. Perhaps you've a balcony seat on cat fights. Or worse, the spine-chilling warble of a nest of innocents being attacked. Primal and raw, it all comes in the night. Unfiltered. The world as it is.*

NATIONAL BLUEBERRY MUFFIN DAY (JULY 11): *Be rebellious: Make blueberry pancakes, instead. Lift a fork to so much joy jam-packed inside a tender globe of berry, nature's tiniest juice balloon. Beholding joy, prayer distilled.*

BLESSING 10: *The Sisyphean summer task: Hour upon hour yanking weeds from the garden, where pushing and shoving among roots is getting out of hand. And weeds could win Best of Show. The meditation: What a gift to weed from your life whatever gets in the way of reaching toward the heavens.*

BLESSING 11: *Ponder the wisdom of Celia Thaxter, 1835–1894, New England poet and author of* An Island Garden: *"In this hour divinely fresh and still, the fair face of every flower salutes me with a silent joy. . . . All the cares, perplexities, and griefs of existence, all the burdens of life slip from my shoulders and leave me with the heart of a little child that asks nothing beyond the present moment of innocent bliss."*

BLESSING 12: *There's no substitute for a summer's rain. No rinse of all the earth that so revives what dwells here. Summer's rain is balm, soothes parts of us we didn't even know were hurting. Till we hear the whoosh, or pit-a-pat. And then the healing washes over us.*

BLESSING 13: *Summer shower's postlude: the rainbow. Boils down to basics, pure and simple: light + water (in the form of rain or, in a pinch, straight from the hose) = arc of infinite color. That we might always see through to every moment's miracle.*

BLESSING 14: *Night prayer: Listening for rain in dry season, hear the rumblings of far-off thunder, like growling from the woods. Through the half-slept night, it's not unlike keeping one ear perked for a fevered child, down the hall. We don't doze so soundly when we worry about the blessed things whose watch we keep. And we keep watch on parched and thirsty earth. When infusion comes, we bow down in deepest gratitude.*

The Weightlessness of Summer
On Savoring

It comes without notice, like butterfly wings that waft before your face, your cheeks, the bump that ends your nose.

You catch the barest shift of breeze, a fluttering of light, you look up, you realize: Something sacred just passed by. It came from who-knows-where, but along the way, it surely graced me.

And so it is with summer, with those wisps and darts of weightless wing. With the moments when the heaviness of all-year-long is suspended, when breeze blows through the screen, garden leaves flutter, light practically sparkles, and you feel your shoulders drop their heavy load.

It comes when dinner isn't rushed and isn't quite at dinner-time. But rather wends its way to the table at, oh, minutes shy of nine. And when the table is not the inside one, but rather the old slab of door with wobbly legs, the one that stands and beckons from the summer porch, the room with screens, the room lit partly by candlelight and moon, and partly by fireflies blinking by.

June Field Notes: Big news this month is the solstice; summer, north of the Equator, and winter making its debut down south.

It isn't always here, that weightlessness that marks the essence of summerness. There are days and hours when the rush is still the same, when the thick soup of humidity slows you to a crawl, but still you're dashing here and there, with no hope of long tall drinks of lemonade, or feet propped up on summer-splattered pillows.

But that, I think, is what makes for the deliciousness of summer when it comes, when you catch it, when you're standing at the sink and you don't mind that it's late, because the stars are out, and you intend to amble back outside, to sit and stare into the heavens, to not worry one iota about bedtime or the ticking of the clock toward midnight.

Amid a week of hustle and bustle, and birthdays and gosh-darn tornadoes, summer found me, caught me unawares, wrapped me in its gentle fold, beckoned me, a crooked finger curling inward, "Come, come, savor what my season offers."

And so, I did as told.

I sliced a fat tomato, pinched a stem of basil from my kitchen window box. I sank my teeth into a peach, let the juice drip down and splatter in the sink.

I opened windows, welcomed in the cool night air. I pulled my summer nightgown from the drawer, didn't mind that it had holes, was torn where lace meets buttons. I love that old lacy thing, have held it together with broad white satin ribbons, stitched and re-stitched it, but will not throw it out. Nothing says summer's eve quite like that old white cotton gown, now quirkily ventilated after twenty-some years.

It's midnight sun, up North Pole's way, and the longest light of the year, from way on-high clear down to the globe's full-bellied

I've a sweaty pitcher of pure clear water in the fridge. It's aswim with lemons by the slice and sprigs of mint, both leaving the barest essence of orchard and garden in my glass, and in my every gulp.

All over the house I've tucked old milk pitchers and creamers and itty-bitty glass bottles with pickings from the garden. It's my Friday act of benediction, renewing the vows of beauty from the climbing rose, the catmint, and just this week, the yarrow and hydrangea now in bloom.

But that's just stage-set.

Where summer settles best is in the soul. In the part of you that remembers not to worry for the moment. To soothe the long ragged edges. To breathe.

midline. * The moon that shines amid all this light is most com-
monly known as *Full Strawberry Moon*, or *Rose Moon* or *Hot*

AND THE NEST CAME TUMBLIN' DOWN
On Life Lessons

THE WINDS THRASHED THE OTHER NIGHT. And the rains did, too. Came down hard and heavy like nails from up above. Pelting nails.

On nights like that the trees bend and toss. Make you forget, nose pressed to glass, watching, staring, gasping right out loud, that trees are made of wood not paper.

Makes you wonder, on nights like that one, how the wild things survive. How the dawn comes, and the dewdrops glisten. How the birds shake off their sodden feathers, fly again.

Only, sometimes, they don't.

You tiptoe out in the morning, survey the world that's yours as the light comes up, casts its gold-drenched illumination like a blanket rolling toward the west. Your naked toes drink in the bath that is oozy lawn—two parts mud, one part grass.

You count the fallen things: The poppies pummeled, crepe-paper petals strewn, so much sad confetti; the peonies waterlogged

---

Moon, so named because the ones doing the naming knew this as the short sweet season for plucking plump juicy strawberries

and dripping, necks bent, noses pressed into the earth, fuchsia washrags in the end, their short season cut even shorter.

It is all the heartache you come to know, come to weather, when you love a patch of earth year after year after one disaster or another.

But then, sometimes, some heart-breaking times, you stumble on a fallen something that draws you to your knees. That draws a gasp.

It's not something you see maybe more than once a lifetime. It's not something you want to see. Not tumbled to the ground anyway. Not tousled, cracked. Before your toes and eyes.

Not when it's a nest, a perfect robin's nest, all mud-daubed, sticks and stems on the outer rim, for stability. And tucked within with grasses finer, softer, where the eggs will gently lay.

Where the eggs are now, as you've stumbled upon it. Where the eggs, two of them at least, still are perfect ovoid realms of possibility.

But the third is cracked. And you can see straight inside, to flesh and blood and little bird, formed and forming. Till the winds and rain and tumbling came, that is.

And there's no mama robin in sight. And you can't hear her either. Can't hear her mournful cry. For she has lost her nest, and babies too.

And you can't bear, quite, to swallow all of this. To make sense of this.

How so perfect a construction can be tossed and whipped by winds and rains and trees that bent like paper.

---

*from the fields. * It's a big month for beastly constellations, with Lion and Dragon and Bears, oh my! Leo, upturned, is standing on*

My mama was the one who found it. She's the one who knows her trees, her wild things, by heart. She lets no day dawn without her keeping close watch. She makes it her job to be the caretaker of all this wonder.

And so, of course, it was on my mother's early morning rounds, the morning after the nasty noisy storm, that she found the nest and eggs that tumbled down.

In my mama's book of rules, you do not leave a sacred something lying there abandoned. As if a discard.

There are no discards when it comes to nature. Only lessons to be learned. And mercy studied.

So my mama lifted it, the nest and all its eggs. Slipped it in a bag, and brought it here, to where I type.

Left it lying beside my keyboard, so I, too, could study its perfection. Its heartbreak. Its potential so abruptly wrenched from the safety and sanctity of the mighty oak's gnarled limbs.

I take these lessons from above quite to heart. I am my mother's daughter, after all.

I don't take it lightly that I am blessed to peer inside a mama robin's grassy labors.

I am again and again enchanted by the brilliant know-how of the birds, how they know to make the nest just so, sturdy on the outside, soft and soothing where the babies would have hatched.

I muse, of course, on how all of us are born knowing the fundamentals of construction—how it is, at least, we build our nests for the ones we hatch and love.

I consider, too, the emptiness of that mama robin's belly. How

---

his head. Ursa Major, the Great Bear, is best known as the home of the Big Dipper, and you'll find the handle doubling as the big

she must be longing still to press against the warmth of those bright blue eggs, where perhaps she felt the stirrings of the life within.

There is much to learn contemplating how mud and sticks and grass combine to build a nest. And how the wind and rain and bending trees could toss it all away.

I consider the thud that must have been, when the nest came tumbling down, stopped hard against the ground. And how that thud echoed in the hollowed heart of that blessed mama robin.

Once again, lessons left for me to learn. Laid before me by my very own Mother Nature.

---

bear's tail. Little Bear, or Ursa Minor, is where you'll find Polaris, the North Star, the guiding light that's long pointed the way for

RESURRECTION FARMER
On Harvesting Wisdom

WHEN I PLANT MY FOOT ON FARM SOIL, I feel a deep-down rumble. It is rather like a vein is opened up, and something of the earth courses through me. I grasp the hard, back-breaking work, but I feel the poetry.

A farm is elemental. It is pure. It is loamy soil teeming with lessons worth sinking your hands into, getting muddy. It's earth and sky, and hard-won curriculum in between.

It's ancient. It's eternal.

You cannot speed up the germination of a seedling. You cannot make it rain. But you can sow seed. And you can hope. And you can, God willing, make it on your own. Feed yourself, your children, the good folk down the road. At least that's the way it's supposed to be. That's the beauty and the tragedy all at once.

It is you and God, down on the farm.

You have entered, I do believe, into a holy equation that depends on sun and rain and soil. Too much, too little, and all is lost. Days and weeks and months of labor, of getting up at dawn, of

---

*all who journey through the midnight hours. * By now, all birds have settled into their summer residences, and you might catch*

sweat rolling down your nose and muscles aching. Of praying. On your knees begging for the rain clouds to come on, to bring the benediction that just might be a quarter inch of rain.

It is, I do believe, a hands-on PhD in all the truths of life. Birth and death and resurrection, sometimes. Anticipation. Heartbreak. Hallelujahs.

For a city girl (with ancestral farmer roots), I've long looked to farms for wisdom. As always, I found it not long ago, on a day I was blessed to turn my old station wagon down a gravel lane, where the corn gave way to a place called Beauregards Farm.

I was out walking there—not far from the old white farmhouse, the tall-as-scarecrow sunflowers, and the sagging barn—with a woman who is now a farmer, a woman who turned to farming in the fallow years after the death of her firstborn, a soldier home on leave from the Iraqi war. When he'd died, drowned in a pond when his hand-me-down Ford Escort missed a bend in a country road in blackest night, the soulful farmer told me she thought she'd never breathe again. Might as well have buried her, too, she said, in the old cemetery where the sun bakes down between the cornfields.

It wasn't till she dumped some throw-away plant in the ground, watered it, watched it bloom, that it dawned on her—after four long years—that she was once again noticing beauty. Maybe, she thought, she could try her hand at what she came to know as resurrection farming.

Plant her sorrows in the earth, she figured, harvest something beautiful, something lasting, from her nearly seven acres. And

*fledglings tumbling to the ground as they try to take to the skies in fumbled first flights. * Fireflies blink on. Bullfrogs and crickets add*

besides, she told me, climbing to her porch swing, she couldn't stand to be indoors anymore, "nothing could contain my sorrow, only the outdoors."

So she signed up for farmer school, and named her farm after Beau, the *GQ*-handsome kid, a twenty-one-year-old Marine corporal stationed in Kuwait, who'd climbed every tree on that farm's wide-open landscape, learned to drive there, went off to war from there.

She plowed through grief, all right. Coaxed beauty from the barren fields. Found resurrection, after all. And you couldn't help but notice.

One of her farm-school teachers put it like this: "[She] reminds me of a quote from Elisabeth Kubler-Ross: 'People are like stained-glass windows. They sparkle and shine when the sun is out, but when the darkness sets in, their true beauty is revealed only if there is a light from within.' She has had terrible darkness set in, and has shone even more beautifully with her amazing light from within."

As we walked the fields that day, I listened hard to my farmer-philosopher friend, soaked up a few hard-won truths.

"The more I planted, the more I grew, the better I became," she said, distilling one of her more lasting wisdoms, one that might apply far beyond her farm.

And then, not ten steps from the hen house, right before us where the Queen Anne's lace was trampled, lay the head and the feathers of what had been one of her twenty-three "Stepford chickens," as she calls the flock.

alto and soprano to the night-song chorus. And cicada, depending on where the summer falls in the noisy throng's thirteen- to

Just like that, a weasel, she figured, came and snatched a bronze-feathered hen. She crouched down, the farmer did, stroked the feathers, cursed the weasel, and then walked on. Said she'd be back to bury the dear thing. It was just another moment on a farm.

Heartache comes in spoonfuls all day long. You get used to heartache, I suppose, because you know there just might be a hallelujah around the next bend.

And on this farm, this resurrection farm, the deepest grief gave way to something lasting, something beautiful. Proof that holy earth births undying promise.

---

seventeen-year cycle, can reach a deafening ninety decibels, about as loud as a train whistle trumpeting only five hundred feet away.

PRAYER FOR A CAMPER
On Keeping Watch

DEAR MOTHER GOD OF WOODS AND TANGLED ROOTS, of see-through lakes, and dawn's first light, of moonbeams drooling on the meadow grass, and birdsong waking up the day,

I have delivered to you my precious child, my tender heart, brave heart. He is yours now, for two whole weeks, yours to hold, to guide along the trails in deepest darkest night, yours to wrap your arms around in those shaky moments just before the sleep comes, when thoughts drift home, when home feels faraway and hollow fills the void.

He is yours now as he leaps off the dock into soft-bottomed sandy swimming hole. He is yours as he climbs the ropes and buckles onto that shiver-me-timber woodsy trick, the zip line. He is yours as he climbs endless dunes and jumps for dear life. Hold those ankles straight, dear Mother Watcher God. Keep those bones from cracking into twos. Keep bees away, and while you're at it, please shoosh the darn mosquitoes. Ditto poison ivy.

July Field Notes: The incandescence of July glows, in good measure, from Full Buck Moon, so noted by the namers of the

Perhaps, too, you could drift down into the dingy cabin—he's in No. 6, in case that helps—and tap him lightly on the shoulder, whisper in his ear: "Don't forget the sunscreen. Slather on the OFF!" And when he loses things, say, the water bottle, or the flashlight, maybe just maybe you could guide his searching little hand to the very secret spot where said essentials are playing hide-n-seek.

Dear Mother God of star-lit dome, of lake breeze, of rustling in the cottonwoods, you now tend my first-time camper, you hold him to your moss-carpeted bosom. I pray you open up the woods to him, reveal to him the mysteries of your quiet ways, and your crashing-booming majesty.

For two short weeks, we've unplugged him just for you. He's all yours now. He has drawn in a deep cleansing breath, shaken off his deep-woods worries, and surrendered to all the glories you have to offer him.

Tap his tender heart. Unspool for him the depth of confidence that's buried where he doesn't always know it dwells. Allow him to emerge from these woods, from these weeks along that crystal lake, from romping with the troupes of boys and abiding by generations-old rules of woodsmen's games, knowing just a bit more solidly how much he brings to this blessed world.

If so inclined, please be there when the hour comes, at last, for him to light his torch and lift it high—to illuminate not merely his way, but, as well, the twisting paths of all of those who walk beside him.

Hold him tight, dear Mother God, when he needs a squeeze,

---

moons because now's the month when new antlers sprout from bucks in velvet-coated branches. It's also known as Hay Moon, or

and be the wind beneath his wings when he glances down and sees that he is soaring, gliding where the eagles glide.

That's pretty much the whole of it from here on the home front, where I've nothing left to do but turn to you and trust with all my heart.

Thank you, Mama God, God of dappled afternoon light, God of pit-a-pat of summer rain, God who wraps the campers in her arms, and holds them safe and blessed ever after.

---

*Thunder Moon, as celestial turbulence strikes percussively with midsummer crash and boom. * This is a supernal month to view that starry-eyed archer, Sagittarius, smack dab in the bull's eye of the Milky Way. Look down low, near the horizon, if you're north of the Equator. You'll find him shining there, bow arched and aiming. And, indeed, these are the Dog Days. So named because the dog star, Sirius, does the darnedest summer disappearing act: The bright light of Canis Major appears to sidle up to the sun as the season's sizzle strikes, and, for forty days, Sirius rises and sets shoulder-to-shoulder with the solar orb. By daylight, the old dog is lost in sun's glare; by nightfall, off duty. Ancient Romans and Egyptians were convinced Sirius, in cahoots with the sun, was to blame for heat and drought, from July 3 to August 11, so they leashed his tag to the string of dogged days. The Delta Aquarids meteor show peaks in late July, so be on the lookout for heaven's sparks igniting against the jet-black slate. One last*

BEYOND THE DOUBLE DOORS
On Love, Tenderly

MAYBE YOU'VE BEEN TO THAT PLACE. The invisible line where someone you love is in the hands of strangers you've not seen before. And, at the very last instant, the strangers turn to you, just barely, more like over their shoulder they remember you're there, call out, almost a bark, "This is it."

So you, quick, grab a kiss. You gulp and you stand there, just this side of the big swinging doors. With barely a whoosh then a clunk, the doors open. Then swallow the someone you love.

And you are left standing there. Trying not to worry. Trying to chase all the thoughts from your head. The ones that sometimes bang around in your brain. Sometimes make you afraid.

Or, not quite so dreadfully, there are the gallumps in your heart. The ones that forever remind you—even though you are now silver-streaked, and drive your own car—that the someone they just took from you, she is the one who long ago kissed your knees when you banged them. She alone knew how to scramble

---

skylight: Jupiter, the jumbo planet, begs your nocturnal attentions—especially when it's in line for its closest encounter with

your eggs the way you liked them best. She, too, was the one who, that hot summer night when you were nine, maybe ten, sat in the dark with you, your backs against the door of the fridge. And together you nibbled away at the pan of fudge she'd slipped from the shelf where it set for an hour or so, after she'd poured in the cream and followed the steps on the little blue box.

You don't quite line up those thoughts, one after the other. It's more like it all comes at you in a wadded-up ball. And as you watch the back of the big double door swing finally shut, sealed, you turn, all alone, and you realize how much you really are helpless.

There's only so much we can do for the ones who we love. We are, in the end, passersby in this play. There are times, and there are places, where we can't be and can't go.

So we wad up our worries and prayers, and we get through the hours till we can be there again. Can be the one to put cool washcloth to head. Can hold onto an arm. Can dial the brothers—far away—give them the word: She's out from the OR. I've talked to the surgeon. She's resting. She'll be all right soon.

And again, you sit by her side. You wait for the flutter of eyes. You wince as you see the arm you've long known and long held, now puffy and bruised, all sorts of tubes running under a gown that's starchy and doesn't stay closed.

You remember, your mother—who to you is so much a part of your story, your ups and your downs, your wings and your clodhopper feet—you remember she is, like all the rest of us, bones and flesh, veins and lumps that need to be cut and removed.

---

lively planet Earth (an ever-shifting occurrence, depending on the year). Only love planet Venus, dubbed "morning star" or "evening

If you're like me, most of the time we prefer to think of our mothers—and all those we love—as well beyond bones. We are not so much accumulations of tissues and cells, we like to pretend, as we are long-spinning spools of story and myth.

We are narrative arc. We are themes that recur. We are climax and denouement. We are character, deeply nuanced, and, more often than not, rather predictable. We stick to our lines. Some of us work hard at refining and raising our sights. Some of us get stuck in a rut.

But always, we are eager to turn each page. To see where this story is headed. To find out if, ever, we say what we mean, and we get at the truth.

Sometimes, it's sitting there at a hospital bedside that we are most keenly aware of just how deeply we're tied. And how tender our hearts are for the one who is lying there, listless and dopey on drugs.

Sometimes what they do beyond the double doors is stir up our souls. Rejiggle the plot. Lay out the players, starker than ever.

The one they return to us, we remember, is not, and will not be, here forever. And so we move with more care, and more purpose, as we tend to their wounds, put cool sips to their lips. And kiss them goodnight in the tenderest way.

---

star," depending when she glides onto the nighttime stage, shines more brightly. * Down yonder, milkweed's in bloom, a sumptuous banquet for monarch butterfly. Blueberries ripen. Kitchen gardens beg for plucking. Thistle plants begin to seed, so goldfinches gather thistledown for upholstering their nests. Fall migration begins, as early birds head south. Raccoons, skunks, and opossums dig up and dine on turtle eggs.

Peekaboo with Cheddar Moon
On Chasing Wonder

I DANCED WITH THE MOON LAST NIGHT. No, really I did. Actually, it was more peekaboo than anything. But we were a pair, the moon and I.

He pulled, I followed.

It started, like many a duet, without me seeing him coming. He tapped on my shoulder from out of the midnight's deep blue.

I was driving toward home in what seemed like the dark of night, through the woods, actually, when suddenly the road took a rise. There he was, wide and ready as could be. Orange. So orange, I blinked for a minute there, not quite sure what I was seeing. There was something huge and round and the color of grilled cheese, just over the treetops. One minute I saw it, the next it was gone.

Had I not been a girl with my hands on the wheel, I would have rolled down the window, gawked. Had I not been a girl who

August Field Notes: Full Sturgeon Moon—or Green Corn Moon, or Grain Moon—spills across the eighth month, when fishing

does not believe in aliens, I would have thought we were being invaded. By a big wheel of cheddar.

Now, it's not every night that the moon is bright orange, and it's not every night that it calls you by name. But that moon, it called me. I heard it.

If the moon is a magnet, and I think it must be, it sucked me straight to the water's edge. I got as close to that moon as the land would allow me. And if I'd had even less sense than I already don't, I'd have jumped in that lake and slapped through the water.

It took my breath away, that big beautiful moon. Took it away in a way that, once again, felt elemental. Felt essential. I was just me, little me, and I was pulled through the night, through the glow, by something that never got closer.

To dance with the moon, to play catch with a raindrop, to give names to the flowers, to whisper to worms, is to let down all those things that keep us apart. It is to whirl in the zydeco jig of creation. To say we belong to the same riotous, marvelous, wonder-filled notion.

Once I'd caught sight of that moon, that glorious moon I had dubbed Cheddar Moon—knowing enough to know all moons have a name, and this was a moon I was deeply being drawn to—I pressed my right foot a little bit nearer to the torn mat under my pedal. I was driving a bit like a woman late for a date. I was afraid by the time I caught up, I might miss him. And this was a dance I was not sitting out.

---

tribes headlined the news that sturgeon ran plenty in the Great Lakes and Lake Champlain. Some tribes called it Red Moon,

As I hurried to get there, past a mile or two of trees and old houses, I thought it quite sad all the windows I passed that hadn't a clue of the moon playing out there.

That moon was a sly one, a sleek one; it did not bare its face to just any old house. It was too low in the sky for most of the folks who were turning out lights, going into bed, missing the peekaboo game.

But I knew. That moon was playing with me. And I, overcome, played along. When I got to the place where the road was no longer, I simply pulled to the curb, locked the car, and started to walk through the night.

I wasn't afraid. Not much anyway. I was going, after all, to play with the moon. The moon, I knew, was watching. Who ever heard of a curly-haired, half-century-old lady stricken while chasing the moon?

And then I got there. Got to the water's edge, where the moon was melting all over the water. I stood there, little me, neck bent, head back. My eyes, I'm certain, reflecting the moon.

I heard the slap of the lake against rocks, against pier. I felt the sand through my toes. I watched as the orange drained out of the moon. The higher it inched, the less cheddar it got.

Mostly, I stood very still. I breathed and I basked in the ooze of the moon on the water. The peekaboo game had finally ended. The moon, as it hung there, was bold and unblinking. No shy suitor, this one. It would have beamed beyond daybreak, I'm certain. But, at last, I bid it good night.

---

*as when August's whole orb rises, it glows burnt red through sultry haze. * The night sky is particularly theatric with meteoric*

By the time I got home, it was a plain old white gibbous moon. It was still a fine moon. But it wasn't a cheddar moon. The cheddar moon, just out for a while, had called me to play. And I answered.

streaks as Perseid's summer shower offers the best such show of the year, with as many as fifty to one hundred shooting stars

THE CROOKED WAY HOME
On the Long and Winding Blessing

W E TURNED LEFT, NOT RIGHT. We turned away from straight roads, roads that did the job, connected the dots, got you where you needed to be, did not dillydally.

We wanted none of that. We wanted to wiggle our way through the state that pretends it's a mitten. We wanted nothing of straight angles, straight shots, sensible directions.

I'd waited a month, driven 366 miles, to get to the boy in the woods, the boy I'd been missing, the boy who'd hiked the whole of Isle Royale, 120 bone-breaking miles.

But really, we'd waited for years, for it just to be him and me and a whole day in front of us. Years past, all sorts of roadblocks got in our way. Surgery. A torn-apart kitchen. Other drivers who preferred the direct route.

Not us. And not this time.

We wanted to soak up the joy of being together. And we chose to do that the slow way. We chose the gray squiggly lines on the

---

per hour streaking across the black-velvet curtain. The Big and Little Dippers move to center stage. And Neptune orbits closest

map. The ones my copilot defined thusly: "It's not gravel, and it's not dirt, and that's all I can say about it."

So only a few times did the pebbles spin out from under our tires, and that was because, once again, we were, oops, getting un-lost, righting our wrongs, needing the side of the road. For the most part, we stuck to two lanes, paved, with the occasional splash of yellow dashing the middle.

The whole point was to meander. To be not in a hurry. Not racing toward anywhere or anything. To be driven only by intuition or a whiff in the air that someplace worth seeing might be just down that road over there.

It was to be reminded, more than a few times, that intuition sometimes steers you clear to where the road up and dead-ends. Exactly the opposite of where you thought you were going. But once there, hey, you meet really nice folk who give you a map, turn you around, and offer a big cup of water besides.

After a while we got to calling our route "the pie way," for all the pies we seemed to be piling on the car seat behind us. We had cherry, of course. And blueberry too. Lattice-top, sprinkled with big chunks of sugar. Like the ice storms that swirl through these parts, come November through April some years.

It got to be rather a moveable feast, but then we were, for a while, in Hemingway country. Hemingway summered at one of the lakes, a crooked old lake called Walloon, which happened to be in our path. That's where we picked up that sweet cherry pie.

With every stop, practically, came a story.

And in between, we filled in with our own. Ours was a car

---

to Earth in summer's latter days, but it's not a naked-eye planet,
meaning you'll need to grab your binoculars to drink in its icy

with the sound of no radio, no tunes, just the stories from camp from my copilot. We squeezed hands once or twice and we cried, or at least I did, listening to all that he told. Hearing the knowledge he picked up in the woods, on the trail that "humbled" him, his word. His wisdom.

And that was the trip that we wanted.

And, oh, the sights from the gray roads . . .

For every farm stand where we pulled onto the gravel, there were six others we passed. And one of us sighing, each time. Why, we saw a field growing nothing but sunflowers. And, darn, that we didn't turn back.

If there'd been a show at the Cherry Bowl Drive-In, we would have turned there, where a six-foot aluminum hot dog, one dripping with all of the fixins, marked the concessions.

It was all the joy of the journey.

There aren't many days that shake you from sleep, shout, "Wake up, take all the time in the world today." Sometimes you have to make those days happen.

You have to fight off the urge to do things the straight way. To get home at a sensible hour.

We came home the crooked way, me and the boy I so love. All in all we drove 455 miles. But that was really only 89 more than the straight way. If you measure in miles.

If you measure in joy, though, it was twice as long, and ten times as deep.

Long as I live, I will never forget: The fellow in the fix-it truck who pulled onto the gravel because he saw all the pointing of

---

blue. * Hummingbirds hover at fever pitch. Flocks of nighthawks punctuate the skies, per definition, through the night. Warblers fingers there at the gas station where we'd stopped for directions; he figured we were lost, thought he'd offer his part in getting us home.

I'll not forget the pie lady who laughed, and then blushed, when I asked if she minded me taking a picture of her beautiful, beautiful pies.

I'll not forget the glow of the sun setting like copper as we drove through the stretch with the steel mills.

I'll not forget the skip in my sweet boy's heart when we rounded the bend, well past nightfall, and there at the curb were his papa and up-too-late little brother.

I'll not forget the long sweet embrace that came at the end of the crooked way home. Sometimes you just need to get there the long way.

---

commence their end-of-summer migration. And monarchs, too, turn en masse toward their Mexican or Californian over-winter outposts, the farthest-flying butterfly on Earth. * In the woods, deer shed velvet from their antlers. And in the meadow, purple coneflower, black-eyed Susan, Queen Anne's lace, and goldenrod embroider brilliant hue and texture. The nests of bald-faced hornet, the original papermaker, grow layer by layer. And twilight hour brings on a sleigh-bell soundtrack with the chirping of the snowy tree cricket, up Northwoods way, and katydids and field crickets stretching clear to the Ozarks.

FROM THE SUMMERTIME
Recipe Box

No-cook summer, the aim. Pluck tomato from the vine. Shake with salt. Consume. Repeat with the sweet pea, the runner bean, the cuke. And who ever met a berry that demanded more than a rinse—if that? Thus, the blueberry slump. A no-frills invention, concocted—lazily, one summer's afternoon—in the produce aisle. Even its verbs invoke indolence: dump, splash, dash . . . spoon and lick. With lick, though, comes a sudden surge of gusto.

Blueberry Slump

(As instructed by a friend bumped into by the berry bins; though long forgotten just who that was, the recipe charms on, vivid as ever.)

Yield: 1 slump

> 2 pints blueberries dumped in a soufflé dish (fear not, that's as close as we come to any sort of highfalutin *cuisine Française* around here)
>
> Splash with 2 to 3 tbsps. fresh lemon juice
>
> Cinnamon, a dash

In another bowl, mix:

1 cup flour

1 cup sugar

1 stick butter, cut into pea-sized bits

(Baker's Note: Add a shake of cinnamon, and make it
vanilla sugar, if you're so inspired. I usually am. All you
need to do to make your sugar redolent of vanilla bean is
to tuck one bean into your sugar canister and forget about
it. Whenever you scoop, you'll be dizzied by high-grade
vanilla notes.)

* Spoon, dump, pour flour-sugar-butter mix atop the
  berries.

* Bake at 350-degrees Fahrenheit, half an hour.

(Oh, goodness, it bubbles up, the deepest berry midnight
blue. Looks like you took a week to think it through and
execute. Ha! Summer in a soufflé dish. *Sans soufflé*.)

* Serve with vanilla ice cream. But of course.

Tiptoe out to where you can watch the stars, I was tempted
to add. But then I quickly realized you might choose to
gobble this up for breakfast, lunch, or a late summer
afternoon's delight. In which case a dappled patch of shade
will do.

Autumn

Season of Awe

Autumnal (or September) Equinox

*At the appointed hour—the hour of equinox—the sun slides
into absolute right angle to Earth, its beams falling straight
onto the Equator. Not angled north or south. Sharp-cornered.
It's equal light for all. Until the morrow, when the sun glides
south, and north moves into shadow. No matter how you
cut it, one season steps aside, another takes the stage. And
the casting's mirrored on either side of the Great Equatorial
Divide. Autumn is upon us to the north, as spring glides in on
the southern edge of Earth's dividing line. The date of equal
night and day—the second such alignment of the year—is on
or near September 22.*

Autumn's Wonderlist

it's the season of . . .

inflamed twilight sky, rosy-streaked, purple-bruised, ablaze with setting sun . . .

jolly pumpkins punctuating farmer's field . . .

the last aster, alone and proud, amid the shriveled diminishment of what had been the summer's shiningest hour . . .

the lonely cry of the unseen geese's night-crossing . . .

molasses light pooled across the windowsills, puddling onto hardwood planks . . .

pomegranate, impaled and gutted to reveal its belly's cache of garnet-seeded gems . . .

golden-glowing woods . . .

old quilts and thick bed covers, unearthed from their long summer's nap . . .

scribble your own here:

A COUNT-YOUR-BLESSINGS CALENDAR:
Blessed Be Autumn, Season of Awe

IN THE CHRISTIAN CALENDAR, ORDINARY TIME CONTINUES, punctuated with Feast Days, All Saints' and All Souls', chief among many. Advent comes as autumn turns toward winter. We kindle lights amid the blanketing darkness. We await the Holy. In the Hebrew calendar, harvest time brings the Days of Awe, the holiest of holy days, from Rosh Hashanah, the Jewish New Year, to Yom Kippur, Day of Atonement, and on to Sukkot, Feast of Tabernacles, the harvest celebration where we wrap ourselves in the whole of Creation and God's abundant glory. From the golden glowing autumn light to the morning's brisk first breath, this is indeed the Season of Awe.

Here, fourteen blessings to amplify the awe.

AUTUMNAL EQUINOX: *Blessed be the golden days and star-stitched nights of autumn. Blessed be triumphant blast of light, and jewel-toned tapestry, as the Northern Hemisphere lets out its final hallelujah before deepening, drawing in. And bless those among us who are wide-eyed to the wonderment.*

BLESSING 2: *Now's the interlude when leaves drop their drab summer-worn green for jaw-dropping amber and gold, copper and crimson. Air turns wake-me-up chilly. The slant of sun drops in the sky, as we twirl farther and farther away, it is all autumn's call to attention.*

MICHAELMAS, FEAST OF ST. MICHAEL AND ALL ANGELS (SEPT. 29): *Considered "chief officer of Paradise," "vanquisher of evil," Archangel Michael slayed heaven's dragon in a great swordfight. As shooting stars streak across autumn's sky, we remember the sword's flash. And, as the dragon is said to have fallen into a blackberry bramble, we feast on the season's last blackberries while considering the evils we must vanquish from our lives.*

FEAST OF ST. FRANCIS OF ASSISI (OCT. 4): *Contemplate the tenderness of the patron saint of woodland critters, who quelled swallows, tamed a wolf, befriended a cricket, and sang with nightingales. His early disciple, Thomas of Celano, marveled in the thirteenth century: "In everything is a scintilla of the goodness of God, and Francis, 'being completely absorbed in the love of God,' clearly perceived this goodness 'in all created things.' "*

BLESSING 5: *There is faith galore in tucking in a bulb, concentrated life. Setting it just so, roots poking down, shoot facing skyward, where vernal sun will tickle it awake, coax from frozen earth, startle us with tender slips of green. Resurrection, sealed beneath the earth.*

BLESSING 6: *Wrap yourself in the prayerful cry of the cello, the orchestra's autumnal offering. No deeper plea for hope than Bach's "Cello Suite No. 5 in C Minor." Might it be the backdrop to your autumn vespers?*

BLESSING 7: *Behold the piercing, minor-key dissonance, raining from on high. It's the trumpet blasts of geese in Vs. Amid this season of migration, as feathered flocks follow heaven's call, consider the words of John Milton, English poet and polemicist, who said of geese: They are "intelligent of seasons." Oh, that we all would be.*

BLESSING 8: *Some call this "the wabi-sabi season," so defined as the season that pulses with the beauty of sadness and the sadness of beauty, and the breathtaking poetry of imperfection and impermanence. Embrace your own wabi-sabi self.*

ALL SAINTS' DAY (NOV. 1): *A radical thought about saints: We each, all of us, possess sparks of the Divine. Our holiest charge: Kindle the light. Touch one flame to another. Before it darkens. If we each spend one minute, one spark of the day, living beyond our small little selves, fairly soon we've ignited a bonfire.*

BLESSING 10: *Bless the miracle of the monarch, the one of all 24,000 species of butterflies who migrates the farthest. For most of the year, the monarch lives an ephemeral life. Within weeks, it dies. Not so autumn's monarchs, the Methuselah generation— named for the Bible's oldest old man, who lived "969 years" (Gen 5:27). Monarchs born at summer's end live eight months. They exist for one purpose: To fly south, and, come spring, beget the next generation. Who in heaven's name dreamed up such almighty wonder?*

BLESSING 11: *Treat yourself to midnight's moon lace. Tiptoe to a window—or straight under heaven's dome. When the moon is nearly full, behold the moonbeams as they spill. All the earth, in dappled shadow. Better than Chantilly, sure to take your breath away.*

BLESSING 12: *Regard the autumn frost: Miracle of sunbeams captured in wee globes of dew, flash-frozen. Or might it be the cold sweat of dawn's labor, the hard work of night turning to day? Either way, let it take your breath away. First blessing of the day.*

THANKSGIVING: *"Contemplation is life itself, fully awake, fully active, fully aware that it is alive. It is spiritual wonder. It is spontaneous awe at the sacredness of life, of being. It is gratitude for life."—Thomas Merton, Trappist monk, mystic, writer (1915–1968).*

BLESSING 14: *As you begin kindling wicks, come nightfall, consider the honeybees' hard labor to beget the beeswax. It's estimated bees fly 150,000 miles to yield one pound of beeswax. As Bavarian thinker Karl von Leoprechting wrote, in 1855: "The bee is the only creature which has come to us unchanged from paradise, therefore she gathers the wax for sacred services." Ponder that when next you illuminate the darkness.*

GROPING FOR GRACE
On Unfurling Prayer

SLEEP WOULD NOT COME, WAS NOWHERE IN SIGHT. Nowhere in the dark, either. Only the thump-thump of my heart in my chest. And the same up in my head.

I did something I haven't done since, Lord, I can't remember. Oh, I have stashed one in my pocket whenever I or someone I love gets wheeled off to surgery. And I've slipped one down to the bottom of my suitcase. Keeps the plane in the air.

But I have not lay in my bed fingering my rosary in a long, long time.

Yet: through the ages, the fingering of small beads is nothing unusual. Nothing new.

Before there were therapists, there were stones at the side of the river, beans dried in the breeze, rosebuds, too, curled into tight little knots there under the late summer sunshine.

So too, we who are Catholic grow up with our rosaries. We get one, or at least I did, when I was old enough to wear little

---

September Field Notes: The equinox, big news of the month, is when the sun, for the second time in a calendar year, glides

white gloves and carry a white straw purse to the pew. The rosary gave me something to do, something to make me look like I knew how to pray there with the forest of tall people, casting shadows, making it dark down where I stood on my tippiest toes, trying for a glimpse of the priest.

I've had ones that glow in the dark (always helpful, always fun for making shapes under the covers, seeing how long you could get it to glow).

I've had a little ring of a rosary, sort of a CliffsNotes of rosaries, a single circle of ten beads and a cross (condensed from the standard long loopy strand of 59 beads and a cross and a medal), that slipped out of my father's pocket when he died, and into mine. It's the one I keep closest at hand.

It's the one I squeezed till my fingers turned white when they threaded the wire into the heart of the man who I love, the man who I married. And when they dug out the cancer from the breast of my mother. And that I would have grabbed, had I known, on the crisp autumn night when the ambulance carried me and my firstborn through the streets of the city, his head and his neck taped to a stretcher. I prayed without beads that night, I prayed with the nubs of my cold, clammy fingers.

Ah, but the one I groped for the other night, it is my glory-be of all glories. It lives in the dark of the drawer beside my bed. Each bead is a pewter rosebud, each joined with the link of a chain. A rather provocative construction, come to think of it.

Rosaries are meant, mostly, to go beyond thinking, and into a deeper place still. Into the place where prayer dwells. True prayer.

---

directly over the Equator, and day and night, light and shadow, are incised into near-perfect halves. And, thus, one season gives way

A complete letting go. Not an asking for this or for that. But for casting your soul to something beyond, letting it light on a breeze. Not unlike flying a kite, really. You let out the string, catch the wind, and then you are soaring. Your kite bobs. It dips and it dives.

So, too, do your prayers. When you pray on the wind. When you pray to the heights and the depths and you're lulled into sleep.

There are spells in our lives that call us back to our very first stirrings. To the God who we know is there like the nightlight that never goes out. I am needing that God right along here. I am clinging to beads in the dark in the night. They're not very far from my pillow. I reach and I grope in the drawer. There they are. Safe in my fist.

Or is it my fist, safe at last, safe in the nest of my beads that carry me places where the wind does the rest?

I just finger the rosebuds, let out the string, whisper the prayer, and I soar.

---

*to the next. Autumn enters, at least in the Northern Hemisphere; spring unfolds down south. * Full Corn Moon, also Barley Moon, presides over the seasonal shift, as it's time to harvest corn, barley, squash, beans, pumpkins and wild rice, staple foodstuffs of the Native Americans who named the moons. * Harvest Moon is the name given to the full moon nearest the autumnal equinox, so either September's or October's moon steals the honors. In two*

TURN AND RETURN
On the Holy Spiral

IT IS HOLY TIME AGAIN.

It is holy time in any autumn hour.

But never holier than on these the Days of Awe—the Holiest of Jewish Holy Days, from Rosh Hashanah, the new year, to Yom Kippur, the atonement day—now mine as much as my beloved's.

Oh, I am Christian—Catholic—through and through.

And, yes, too, I am defined now by the rise and fall of sun, the turning of the moon, the seasons of the planting and the harvest. I kindle lights at sundown on Shabbat. I inhale the spices at the Sabbath's close, at sundown on Saturday, cling all week to the sharp, sweet notes of clove and star anise, allow the lingering pungence to whisper through the weekdays that holy time will come again.

The pause of Shabbat is God's command to put down toil, lift up holiness. Marvel at the simple gifts of consecrated quiet. It is God's promise, too, to fill the holy chalice that is us, leave us thirsting for not a single blessed drop.

---

years out of three, it's September's moon, otherwise the nod goes to October. At the peak of harvest, when every hour counts, that

Yes, there is much poetry that pulses through my heart these days. Passion, too. And much of it is stoked by the prayers I read while I sit in synagogue, turning pages, lost in my own reverie.

It is, to me, all a spiral. The geometry of climbing. The ladder of a soul that reaches toward the heavens.

It is time to turn and return. So says the prayer of each Shabbat. And, the ones for Rosh Hashanah, too.

Even the bread, the challah of these holy days, is freed from its ordinary flat-planed braid, and lifted into ever-rising spiral.

We are told, in prayer and golden-crusted foodstuff, to come back to where it all begins—to turn and return—but take it up a notch. Don't be satisfied with status quo. Don't let dull the sharp-edged hope.

The Days of Awe begin tonight, when the sun slips down beyond the curve of Earth, and the stars turn on, lighting up the night sky.

It is time in this house to turn again to page 82, the lamb-spattered page, the page where cinnamon has fallen, and kosher salt has settled in the gulley of the binding. It is lamb-stew time, the one single recipe upon which this union was begun. Upon which it will, God willing, always rise.

Just home from our honeymoon, in early September of 1991, encamped in an upstairs apartment in a tiny blue-framed house, the man I'd just married opened up the book I'd given him years before, before I ever dreamed I'd be his wife. He settled on the stew that would become our touching-stone. That will be stirred on our stove, as long as there are arms to hold the long, wooden

---

moon's so bright, the day's labor could be finished under moon-light, instead of farmhands being chased from fields as darkness

spoon. To sprinkle leaves of thyme. To chop apple into chunks. To dump in raisins by the cupful.

It is, as we grow year upon year, a sense of coming home. We stir and we remember. We set the plates and pomegranates on the table, and we bow our heads in prayer.

We turn and we return.

It is all about the holy coil that lifts us on our journey. That brings us back, again and again, but never to the place we've been before.

There is, we realize with every passing year, unparalleled beauty in coming round again to that moment in the days, the weeks, the months—the season—when all the world echoes: We've been here before.

And here's your chance to savor it again, to learn again. Or maybe for the first time.

It is holy and sacred, this spiral-marking, and it comes at the moment when my heart is ripe to bursting. When every pore of me wants to slurp the molasses light that's pooling all around.

I am inclined in these Days of Awe to walk wherever I must go. I want to feel my soles slap against the Earth, feel the bumpy acorns, catch the light as it pours through golden-turning leaves.

It's almost as if I can't get enough of the gift: the gift of the spiral, the coming back to the essence—the joy and the beauty, the pure holiness—again.

It is time, now, to close my eyes in prayer. To inhale the holy vapors from my stove, my plate, the spice box.

I can't help but want to leap into the holy rushing waters of

---

drifted in. Usually, the moon rises an average of fifty minutes later from one night to the next, but for the few nights clustered around

this sacred river passing by. It's an upflow, I am certain. And an updraft, too.

I am soaring here, on a spiral fueled with cinnamon and cloves. These are the holy blessed days, the Days of Awe, the days of autumn's rapture.

And I do as I'm commanded: I stand in awe, turning and returning . . .

---

*Harvest Moon, the moon seems to rise at nearly the same time, night after night: just twenty-five to thirty minutes later across the U.S., and only ten to twenty minutes later for much of Canada and Europe. * The autumnal river of migration is at its peak, warblers flying en masse, hummingbirds long south, waterfowl revving their south-bound wings. On the contrary, juncos and white-throated sparrows, so-called snowbirds, move north to settle in for winter.*

WHAT IF . . .
On Untethering Time

I WAS LURCHING TO A STOP, at a light leaping toward red, and that's when the thought was birthed in my head. It had been pulling at me all morning. I felt the weight of it from the moment my eyes opened, let in the dawn's light.

I was having trouble letting go of the great sacred hours of Saturday, Yom Kippur, the Day of Atonement. It had been a day of pure oxygen. I'd had nowhere to be other than prayer. I did nothing worldly. It was as with any meditative pause, when we unbind the tethers of the day-after-day and bathe ourselves in the tide pools of silenced contemplation.

I drove only at the end of the day, when the dark came. All through the daylight, I walked to the place where the prayer was in pews. I walked with my boys; we weren't in a hurry. The little one filled his pockets with acorns, sat off in a corner when we got there, played games with the corns and their caps. My first-born, wrapped in his prayer shawl, stood beside me, sat beside

---

* The woods literally mushroom as rain and cooler nights urge stems and caps from primordial sleeping grounds. Old Man of

me, prayed beside me. Their papa, this year, was far away, back at the synagogue where he'd first wrapped himself in the shawl of his prayer.

We spent enough hours, my boys and I, in the place where the prayer was—coming and going all day—that we followed the arc of the sun.

The morning light, white, filtered through glass the color of cafe au lait, poured in from the east, lit my pages of prayers from the top, spilled toward the bottom.

By late afternoon, the light streaming in from the west was golden. Some in the pews wore sunglasses. I let the sun in without filter, let it practically blind me.

When the sun fell, when the light thinned, the rabbi lit a bright candle. For a few minutes, it was the only light in the great-ceilinged chamber.

Then, it was over and we stepped out into the twilight. Walked home one last time.

It was the light and the words, and the pushing away of the everyday, that drew me into a place where I want to return. The rabbi kept saying Yom Kippur is the one day, the one twenty-five hours of the year, when we brush up closest to God; we taste paradise, he told us. I believed him. I felt the stirring inside me.

I felt the touch of the fingers of God, up near my temples, up where the prayers settle and launch back into orbit. Up where my thoughts rustle like grasses.

I felt time itself transform. It was not a staccato of chocka-block minutes. But, rather a plane with no beginning or end. It

the Woods is one you'd not forget, with wizened tufts across its domed lid, like an old man who hasn't met a razor blade in

147

was a mist that carried me. Took me deep into a place where the world could not enter. It was sacred and slow and without measure. I had no hunger. Other than that of wanting the day to last forever.

And then came the next day. And everything about it, it seemed, was hard. There were breakfasts to make and errands to run. And a whole week ahead. I felt the wallop of Monday galloping toward me.

I was on my way home from the mall where I'd gone to buy knobs for a door that resisted the ones I'd already bothered to try. That's when the words came.

What if?

What if we let go, just for a spell, of all the constraints and let time return to its essence? What if we put out our hands and cupped as much as we could? What if these were our very last hours? What if we allowed each minute to sink deep into our soul?

Would we be racing to malls? Or would we be breathing? Filling our lungs with the warmth of a sun that hasn't gone out yet?

Would we know if a Monday followed a Sunday? Would we care? We have lassoed the moments of time, coerced them into ill-fitting forms.

Oh, I know, I know. We have lives to lead, jobs to fulfill, mouths to feed.

But might we maybe have gone overboard?

Gotten so locked into clocks and calendars that we never, only

---

months. And don't think fungi are merely muted citizens of the forest floor; as fall progresses, so too do mushrooms' rainbow

maybe once a year, and only if we must, tell time we're not paying attention. We are, instead, wholly indulging in the gift of the light and the breeze. We are sinking our hands and our heart and our soul into the timeless. We are digging holes for a bulb, kneading bread dough, rocking our children. We are watching the waves, holding a butterfly, listening to air flutter the leaves of the trees.

The gift of the Sabbath offers that very reality. One day of each week. From sundown to sundown. For years now, I've said I wanted to follow the laws of Shabbat: not drive, not do any labor. Pull into a place that knows no end or beginning. Knows only the light of the sun and the stars and the moon.

What if each day we honor one blessed hour, or one blessed chunk of an hour? What if we give time its due? Not lock it and chain it and wrap it around us.

But rather, allow it to flow through our hands, each sacred drop tasted for all that it is: the closest element in the world to paradise itself.

If we give it a chance.

If we let it sink into our skin, in through our eyes and our ears. If we taste it. If we suck on the marrow of time. If we stop and we marvel. The difference between any one moment and the next might be the difference between life, and life no longer.

Each moment is sacred.

If only we notice.

If only we live as if we grasp the whole of that truth . . .

---

colors: red, orange, yellow, green, blue, indigo, and violet, you can find them all. Roy G. Biv of the woods, indeed.

STARS AND WONDER
On Divine Illuminations,
Above and All Around

W HEN THE SUN SLIPS DOWN TONIGHT, we too will slip away, slip outside.

We'll kindle lights, bless the passage of sunbeams giving way to moonbeams, anoint the cusp of Sukkot, the Jewish festival of joy.

We'll take to the domed cathedral, the one whose holy sanctum arcs beyond our reach, the one papered every night in stars. Itty-bitty, far, far away points of shining light.

It is God's command, on the fifteenth day of the seventh month of the Hebrew calendar, to take to the world beyond our sturdy shelters, the ones of doors and windows, floor joists and heating vents, and taps that spill water with no more than a twist of the wrist.

It is the season of holiness in this house that draws from all the holy wells.

October Field Notes: Full Hunter's Moon—or Dying Moon or
Blood Moon—illuminates October's night. When leaves are falling,

And so, we do as it is written in Leviticus, chapter 23.

We take to our dwelling in the harvest field. We take to our rickety, not-so-sturdy shelter, the one meant to remind us that wherever we dwell, God is our shelter.

At our house it means that, for eight nights, we will take our evening meal out in the screened-in porch, tacked onto the garage, tucked beneath the pines.

It's not quite living up to the Levitican prescriptions. Not quite roofed with twigs and branches, hung with plants that can't be eaten.

But then I'm all for extracting the essence, not getting tangled in particulars.

And the essence here is breathtaking, once again.

We are being commanded to step beyond the comfortable, the heated, the not-so-drafty. We are commanded to immerse ourselves in the world of night, and all its bright and shining wonder.

Stripped of all that we take for granted the other 357 nights of the year, we carry platters and pitchers out to where the chill autumn air runs shivers down our spine, where we twist our legs one over the other as if braided beeswax and do a little warm-up bounce, where we thank heaven for the invention of knitted socks and Levi Strauss's blue jeans.

We watch the flicker of the candle flame dodge and dart upon our flaky-painted, old-door table. And, come the full moon, we'll indulge in no shortage of moonbeams to light our way.

It is this tight-stitched seam between our own bare selves and

---

and game is fattened, the hunter takes to field and stream. It's time to lay in provisions for the long, cruel winter. Because fields

the whole of creation that draws me deep and deeper into the Hebrew calendar, the calendar of so many of our roots.

I hear its echoes through and through my soul.

I am a child of the Earth and heavens. I find myself at once skipping like a schoolgirl full of wonder, and hushed in awe, something like the monks whose vespers follow the unfolding of the holy hours, and the turning of the globe, away from, then toward the sun.

I am humbled by this call to take in the autumnal majesty. To sit beneath the wind-blown boughs, to listen to the acorns plonking on the roof above my head.

And as the stars come on, one by one, as if the dimmer switch is turned, or the caretakers of wonder travel through the heavens, sparking all the star-wicks with their long-necked matches, I am rapt.

It is no less than a commandment of Sukkot that through the roof—called a *skhakh* in Hebrew—we should be able to see the stars.

The point, I do believe: Do not dismiss the divine sparks of light scattered all around, in this case the ones painted on the black cloth of night.

And that's a point that fills me with wonder.

It's too easy—in a world of megawatts and streetlights so bright they wash the city sky in amber glow—to forget to look up. To ignore the constellations, the sky-markers that over the centuries kept sailing ships on course, and that to this day whisper to the flocks of fall's migration just which way to flap their wings and fly.

---

are traditionally reaped in late September, or early October, hunters could easily spy the fox and other critters who came to glean

I stumbled on that latter bit of holiness, the bit about sky-markers and migration, just the other day, and it's one that hinges wholly on the stars that shine above.

I learned, talking to an esteemed author of many books on birds, that scientists have proven the uncanniest of celestial wonders, one that, like October's winds, gives me the shivers.

It seems that in the springtime and early summer, when the baby birds are still tucked safely in their nests, they awake at night, not unlike the squawking species known as baby humans.

Only, bless those feathered things, the baby birds are transfixed by night shadows and the stars above. They are hard at work, those nestlings, stamping in their mind's eyes the patterns of the night sky. Indeed, they memorize the constellations, fix their inner compass to the one lone star that never shifts.

Somehow, within their every fiber, they align their position with the Northstar, and evermore are guided in their migrations, fall and spring, away from or toward that shining beacon. That's how a wee bird, just hatched the spring before, can find its way—untried, untested—from the boreal forests of the north, clear down to where the sun shines warm.

All in cloak of night. All because of one star, fixed at the center of it all. One star guiding the whole rushing river that is the winged migration, flowing north to south and south to north again.

And to think that most nights we don't even bother glancing much beyond the treetops—if at all.

---

from fallen grain. With the threat of winter—and persistent fears of hunger—looming ever closer, Hunter's Moon assumed elevated

And so it is that we are commanded, drawn beneath the night sky, instructed to mind the shining stars.

As if a whisper stirring us, reminding: The Divine is here and there and everywhere.

Sukkot beckons: Were we to step into the holiness of bough and birdsong and rushing wind, we stand to be washed over with a saving grace.

And so it will be. At nightfall, I will leave behind my sturdy house and go to where the winds blow and the starlight flickers on.

I will take a seat at the table in the breezy, chilly place where God, sure and steady, is my shelter, and my peace.

---

honors, a feast day in Western Europe and among North American tribes. * Aquarius, the water bearer, and Pegasus, the winged horse, are the bright lights of October's star map. Pegasus was storied to be Zeus's thundering beast, and the carrier of his lightning bolts. Aquarius, an old man pouring water from a bucket. Both are high overhead as evening's ushered in. The Great Square of Pegasus, considered a landmark of autumn, gallops onto the October night sky, with four stars of nearly equal brightness, in the shape of a baseball diamond, a straight shot east of Polaris, not too far above the horizon. * Autumn colors peak, the woods ablaze in fire colors. Goldenrod, asters, and blazing stars—the jewels of autumn—carpet the wild meadow. * Fall songbird migration is petering to its final notes, but in the Great Lakes, warblers, creepers, wrens, and kinglets are thick in southward flocks. Winter birds settle in; chickadees, nuthatches, woodpeckers, and jays cache for the cold to come. Waterfowl migration—the loon, the Sandhill Crane, the Canadian goose—surges on. In the

THE PLACE WHERE THE PRAYERS COME
On Heaven's Vault

THE PEOPLE HERE FIRST, THE PEOPLE LONG, LONG AGO, the ones who were blessed, who lived off its forests and lakes, the ones whose very skin knew the touch of the divine all around, the ones who gave names to each tree and each dip in the path, they would have had a name for this place. A name that rolled off the tongue.

My name is not so poetic. My name is simple. I call it The Place Where the Prayers Come.

I am pulled there, to the tall grasses that grow in the sand at the edge of the lake, the great lake. I am pulled there like some sort of tide in reverse.

The waves roll in one way. I roll in from the other.

The October sun lures: Come to the place where the lake never stops. Some days it crashes, others it tickles. But the sound is incessant. No matter what else, there is always the play of the water on sand.

*Southeast, bald eagle nest building begins. * Along river beds and streams, woodchucks and beavers stingily scarf as much as they*

155

It's a place where the sky is the dome and the vault is forever. The church has no walls. Its very architecture demands the propelling of thoughts. There's the rustle within, and the catapult beyond. A horizon that's infinite. That has room for whatever flows.

There is no feeling cramped in the pews in this place. You can wiggle your toes in the sand. You can feel like a ladybug, too. Nestled there in the grasses that bob in the sun, play catch with the rays, turn golder than gold. And then dim.

You get caught in the swirl here. In the sounds and the sun and the sand.

There is no sign that's posted. Other than the one about keep off the ice. But that belongs to a whole other season, and I pay no mind.

Still, I notice, time after time, that I'm not the only one called here. There's a sprinkling of others. All of us joined in the hushed and holy communion of publicly dropping our guard, unspooling what lies in our hearts.

There are benches for those who don't favor sand. But me, I bury myself there in the grasses. Like a quail in the rush, I go as small as I can. Against a sky and a God without beginning or end.

It makes me feel wrapped, held in very big arms.

I never stay long. I don't feel the need to. The fuel that comes there, in the place of the prayer, it is rather intense. It fills me quite fully. And it lasts.

Till the whisper comes once again. Come to the prayer place. Come to the place where the prayers come.

It's as holy a place as I know.

---

can before their long winter's nap. Squirrels and chipmunks do the same, though the squirrel won't snooze the winter away.

DANCING BY MYSELF
On Joyful Abandon

PERHAPS YOU SHOULD KNOW: NO ONE ELSE WAS HOME.

It was an otherwise ordinary morning. The sun was golden, was pouring in in that way that sunbeams, come November, pour like molasses on a tall stack of flapjacks.

The birds, just out the window, were chattering like schoolkids on a bus on a field trip.

I was trying to write. I decided maybe a backbeat would help. My brother, one faraway now, one off in Maine, came to the rescue, as often he does. He knows music, has a collection as eclectic as any I've ever known. Global music is his thing, Africa, Ireland, New Orleans, Brazil, Guinea-Bissau, India. Water drops pouring through copper pipes—he has made it be music.

I slipped in a disc, one he'd once made. Sao Paolo ripped through the speakers, and there on the rug, I was twirling, was clapping, was flowing like some sort of teenager who wasn't afraid, wasn't ashamed, was lost in the bass and the backbeat, and the forest of sound that came crashing my way.

November Field Notes: Full Beaver Moon, or Frost Moon, is so named for the indigenous peoples' task of setting beaver traps

Did I mention that I was alone?

And then as the volume rose, and so too the sense of abandon, it hit me how home—that place that after a while, after we pay some attention, haul in the artwork that stirs us, lace it with blankets and pillows and odd sorts of collections that remind us of long-ago someones or faraway places—home is not only four walls and a roof.

Not at all.

Home is the ultimate intimate relationship we all yearn for. It is the space where we can be naked, and I don't mean without clothes, although that's possible too.

What I mean is it's the place, the rare sanctified place, where we can be the wholeness of who we were made to be. We can pull back the armor, the shields, and the shell.

We can rock. We can spin. We can pound on the floors with our toes.

We can slip into skin that feels at once selfish and stripped of the self. We can indulge in the rhythm of being wholly alive, to the point that we lose track of our selves.

Then, we think, oh my God, please let there not be a reader of meters, who just got a glance in the window.

I've seen it, I've caught it, with children. Tiptoe down in the basement, and there, behind a door that's half-closed, a five-year-old boy is pretending he's there in a stadium. He's throwing and cheering and running the bases all at one time.

And then, the second he sees you've arrived, he flinches and turns into stone.

---

before the swamps froze, in order to ensure a winter's worth of furs. Some, though, say the name is attributed to the busy

The magic is dashed. Is over. Is gone.

It's back to a dingy old playroom where the heat never comes.

When we're home, truly home, and no one is watching, we get to try on our very deep selves. Not deep, mind you, like some kind of a far-reaching thinker, but deep like down to the place where the wires run straight from our soul. Where we are, maybe, as close as we get to the being God once had in mind.

A creature who twirled with all of the rhythm and nuance, and reckless abandon, deserving of a handmade design. An original, in every which way.

What a magnificent thing then if there is one place in the world where we feel back to the womb. Where we allow our home to be more than merely the place where we eat, where we sleep, where we soak in the tub.

How amazing that home is the place where we get to practice. Get a taste of the feel of being, well, completely at home. We can dance, we can sing, we can pretend we're some sort of a hero. We can give speeches, if that's what we please. We can write, and recite, poems. And we don't have to wince or to blush.

For that is the gift that, in the end, we're all seeking. It is Eden without all of the apples. It is, I would think, the point of this whole exercise, really.

It's what we are seeking, time after time, in most every relationship that matters: a place and a space where we don't have to explain. Where we simply can be, can unpeel the layers, and not be embarrassed.

The more we undress, the closer we are to our life's truest

---

*flat-tails' winter preparations, literally making a splash and snaring lunar title. * Even though darkness blankets much of November,*

love. And how blessed it is that the place where we live is, in some ways, as close as we get to that place of total abandon.

No wonder we get through the door with a key that unlocks no other place.

It is a sacred thing, I would insist, to come into a space where we can dance with abandon. Where we can be not diluted, nor half of the plan of the God who imagined us.

But where, with every inch of our skin, and all the room in our heart, we can fill out the shadows and cracks. We can be wholly at home in the soul we were meant to be.

---

with dusk earlier and earlier and dawn later and later, it's the predawn sky that holds the most drama. At certain celestial

SEED SCATTERER
On Sowing in the Fallow Years

SOMEHOW, THE OTHER NIGHT, I swallowed wholly one of the truest truths of growing a thinking child.

Might have been one of the hardest ones to swallow, too.

But in the end, I am convinced, I'm one inch closer to a place that's wiser. Even if the getting there was bumpy going down.

You see, somewhere deep inside my head I thought that passing on the flames you hold most deeply, dearly, was a matter simply of holding up the wick, turning to the ones we nurse, we diaper change, we spoon feed, we wipe off, bandage, and shuffle on their way. The ones whose ears we whisper into, the ones whose shoes we tie, the ones whose pencil grip we help to rearrange. The ones whose papers we are no longer asked to read, for they are thinking now wholly on their own.

To pass the flame, I thought, was merely this: We turn and touch our kindled wick to theirs. And, poof, the burning light continues.

---

*interludes, Venus is unmistakable in the eastern sky, and Saturn rises up from twilight's glare. * All the woods are stripped of leafy*

Only, the other night, deep in thought and conversation at the kitchen table, deep in one of those tête-à-têtes that starts out slow, builds, spirals, and suddenly is way up high on some perch where air is thin, and grip is slipping, I realized that not all flames are so easily lit from soul to soul.

Not when you have, all your life, raised your child to think, to ask, to sift through what he's told, to make his own only that which sinks deep down to a place where what fits is weighed, is looked at from all sides, is held up to the shadow-casting light.

The subject, more or less, was religion. And in this house that's a subject that comes with many threads. We weave here. We are braiders. We sift for golden strands, we entwine. We understand that some are shared, and some are wholly different, depending on whose birth threads we are holding.

More than religious, though, I am of the Spirit. I find God in the scarlet flash of papa cardinal in the snowy boughs, and in the murmurings of the stooped old man who coos to the pigeons. I feel the shiver of the Holy Spirit when I watch the moon shadow play upon the windowpanes, and spill onto the bedclothes that bundle up and over my baby boy.

I whisper the Our Father, but I brush away a tear when lost in prayer on Yom Kippur. I feel the Breath Divine in Hebrew, Latin, or plain-old sidewalk talk. I needn't be in church to know that holiness is near.

And so, it was the burning flame of Spirit that I assumed—no, I counted on it—I'd pass to my firstborn.

As clearly as he got my curly hair, the dimple of his father's

---

glow; bare-boned architecture now fingers the heavens. The forest floor is fed from what's been dropped for weeks; death cheek, I thought the one most precious breath I have, I'd turn and breathe easily, wholly, into my soulful child.

Oh, he had it when he was little. Looked up at me one night, when he was all of two, and asked, "Who puts God to bed at night?"

He had it, just a year ago, when he stood on the *bimah* (that's Hebrew for "altar"), proclaiming the words of the Torah at his bar mitzvah. Brought down the house, I tell you, with his grown-up understanding that clearly sparked the rabbi's imagination.

But now, now he's taken History for Thinking Children, he's heard word of wars fought in the name of God. And philosophies that stretch his mind into interesting new shapes. He is, right now, in this interlude, not so certain anymore.

And as we talked, I ached as the words he spoke fell upon my ears, sifted down to where my soul does all its breathing.

I tell you, it hurt to swallow, and, yes, to breathe.

But he is mine, and that's unshakable, and, besides, I believe I've glimpsed the outlines of that soul. Even if, right now, he calls it something else.

Late that night, tossing, turning, in the way a mother sometimes does, it came to me, the image of the seeds.

I realized that what we do, in the long, long years of planting, is we are merely sowers of the seed. We scatter all life long, the bits of truth, of hope, the few scant things we know.

We scatter as we turn the words, in conversation after conversation. We poke a fertile nugget deep into the soil as we take our children by the hand, show them places and faces unlike the ones they would otherwise know.

---

*to life, the cycle ever spirals, Earth's da capo, "begin again." ** *Monarch butterflies' 2,500-mile transcontinental migration flutters*

We sprinkle seed through the books we read them when we pull them on our lap, turn pages. And then, years later, leave bound offerings tucked beneath their pillow, just in case they find a minute for inhaling thought before they fall to sleep.

And after all the sowing, I realized, we can only stand back. Pray for rain and sunlight. Keep watch on what's out where we have laid our lifetime's crops.

Hmm, is that a little bit of green, poking through the loamy soil? Is that a tendril, reaching for the sky?

We'll not know the harvest for some time. But we will trust that all the planting, tending, praying was not in vain.

Some seasons, what comes up is rich, is plenty, fills the bins. Some seasons, what you put into the ground isn't what comes up at all.

But there will be a reaping. And, God willing, it will be more than you had ever counted on.

That's the way it is when it comes to growing a thinking child. We've no flame to simply light their way, only seeds to scatter on their path, and wait—and hope—for blossoming to come.

---

to a close, as stained-glass wings by the tens of thousands descend into oyamel fir trees in the Central Mexican mountains, or,

NOVEMBER SKY
On Drawing Deep Within

I FIND MYSELF LOOKING OUT OF WINDOWS. LOOKING UP. I'm hiking here and there and everywhere, like a woman starved, trying to fill her belly. Only what I'm hungry for is sky.

There is something particular about November sky that calls me much more often, much more insistently, than the summer months, or even spring.

November sky is haunting, is gray, is roiling when the winds whip, making froth of clouds. We cannot escape.

November sky is vast, is tinted with a wash of winter blue. There is more to see, because less is in the way. Just the bare-boned architecture of the trees, stark, sharp against the canvas of the sky. Sticks poking into clouds, or so it looks from far away, daring sky to burst.

The disrobing's over now. It's limb and bough and twisted trunk. A tree stands alone, telling its solitary story. No encumbrances, no leaves, no frills. Just the bending, arching, reaching limbs, and whatever's fallen too.

---

for monarchs west of the Rocky Mountains, the winged excursion comes to pause in Pacific Grove, California's fog-shrouded

We see it all now. We teeter here on the precipice between the autumn and the winter. Not yet snow sky, but I get the sense it's coming any day.

I could watch all day.

The gray sky for me is one big knitted afghan. I draw it round my shoulders. Hunker down beneath November sky.

It is signal, mostly, that it's time for one and all to go deep, pull in, be ready for the cold winds that will come. Bulbs are buried. Painted turtles sleep along the bank of the lagoon. Even little sparrows, long past nesting, have been collecting bits of cloth, flitting off to somewhere where I think they've knitted their own afghan for the winter.

I, too, go deeper in these days. Pull in. Take my cues from sky. I, too, ready for the winter. Put the gardens all to bed. Haul out the soup pot. Simmer beans and bones, whatever takes the long slow flame, offers up its essence over time, over hours that aren't hurried. Not at all.

But I go deep in other ways.

This is the season, starting now, for introversion. Funny, then—odd, even—that it's the season that the world claims for merriment. Hmm. So maybe that's why, sometimes, for some of us, it's like climbing through molasses to go out and join the crowds.

Maybe if we listened to the sky, we'd be more in keeping with the rhythms deep within.

I believe in seasons. And not because I'm the daughter of Ecclesiastes.

---

*sanctuary of pine and eucalyptus. * Waterfowl migration forges on. Common loons dot the Great Lakes landscape. * Persimmons*

No, not that at all.

I believe in seasons because I believe that Wisdom understood the ebb, the flow, the time to plant, the time to harvest under heaven.

---

ripen on the bough. Witch hazel is the season's last bloom, at least in the northern United States. Mushrooms carpet the wood-lands, ready for foraging. It's the height of deer breeding season, and river otters return to their native range. Days are shorter, nights longer. All the world quiets.

FROM THE AUTUMNAL
Recipe Box

*Soon as that molasses sunlight dribbles in across the
kitchen windowsill, I'm hauling out the pots and pans.
I'm chopping. Stirring. Inhaling deeply. I'm strangling
circulation at my wrists and forearms, dangling bags far
too heavy, too many, as I troll the farmer's market, come
harvest time. Harvest time: When pumpkins delight, and
zucchini threaten to maim with their record-breaking
heft. Pears, piled high, recline, blushing all the while.
And apples by the bushel beg for a root cellar back at
the old homestead. Maybe, just maybe, one last stub-
born tomato ripens on the vine. And, wise to this waning succulence, this savoring, you waste not a drop. You
fill the larder. You relish, indeed you do.*

Aunt Brooke's Cranberry-Pear Relish

Apt, this dish named *relish*. Must be because you can't help
but lick the spoon. You relish it, the relish. Its majesty came
to me by way of my Upper East Side sister-in-law, the so-
titled Aunt Brooke, who, with four hungry boys, knows her
way around the kitchen. She turns out capital-D Delicious,
and her stock-in-trade defense, often: "It's a cinch." This
time, she was straight-talking. Slice, dump, wait. That's
about the whole of it. But what emerges is a pot of

garnet-jeweled deliciousness. And at our house, it's now synonymous with all that's best about the autumn kitchen. We serve it straight through to Christmastime, long as there's a pear waiting to be sliced, and whole cranberries willing to succumb to the cookstove's sultry steam bath.

Provenance: This gem, a family heirloom from Aunt Brooke, a baker extraordinaire, who dabbles splendidly in cooking, and who is known to the world as Brooke Kamin Rapaport. She long ago acquired this from her Great-Aunt Eleanor Serinksy.

Yield: Enough to fill a medium-sized serving bowl (I often double the recipe, since more is always wanted.)

Three Bosc pears, unripened, unpeeled

One package (12 oz.) whole cranberries

1/2 cup water

1/2 cup to 3/4 cup granulated sugar

* The art here is in the pear slicing, so keep the slices slender, allowing the curves to tempt.

* Toss into pot with lid.

* Rinse and dump bag of cranberries atop pears in pot.

* Add water and sugar. Stir but once, taking care not to ravage the pretty pears.

* Cover, cook on medium flame or heat.

* Listen closely. When you hear the pop-pop-pop from beneath the domed lid (about 7 to 10 minutes), turn off heat, and let the magic do its thing.

* Peek in after 15 to 20 minutes. Behold the garnet-hued heap. Stir gently.

* Serve at room temperature, or tuck into the fridge and allow anywhere from half hour to overnight for thickening to occur.

You'll relish it, all right. Might be a side dish on a groaning board, or atop pound cake with a dollop of vanilla-bean ice cream. You'll lick your lips—the very definition of "to relish."

Winter
Season of Stillness

WINTER (OR DECEMBER) SOLSTICE

Once again, darkness blankets the hours. Once again, we've come to longest night—in the Northern Hemisphere. The winter solstice arrives per celestial timekeeper, at the precise moment the North Pole is tilted farthest from the sun, and the shadow cast across the northerly globe is at its longest. In the Southern Hemisphere, of course, it's wholly otherwise, with the South Pole tilted nearest the sun, and southerly daylight at its most protracted. It's all the heavenly concordance of light and shadow. Depending on the crosshairs of your latitude and longitude, the solstice falls on or near December 21.

WINTER'S WONDERLIST

———

it's the season of . . .

kindling candlewicks, flame-by-flame, ancient armament against the inky darkness . . .

traipsing to the woods, hauling home the sacrificial fir to be adorned in paper chains and tinsel, and a lifetime's accumulation of hand-me-down treasures . . .

flour-dusted countertops on the afternoon my grandma's famed cut-out cookies demand to be rolled and baked and iced, then tucked for (short-lived) safekeeping in wax-paper blanketed tins (see recipe, page 91) . . .

scarlet-feathered incandescence aflame against the white-on-white tableau . . .

curling into the couch, under the red buffalo-check blanket, with O. Henry's "The Gift of the Magi," the Christmas classic that forever defines the art of selfless giving . . .

brown-paper packages tied up with red-plaid ribbons . . .

tiptoeing into the dawn to deliver, by Radio Flyer sled, holiday loaves and love notes to all the neighbors' back stoops . . .

making room on the mantle for baby Jesus . . .

scribble your own here:

A COUNT-YOUR-BLESSINGS CALENDAR:
Blessed Be Winter,
Season of Stillness

IN THE CHRISTIAN LITURGICAL CALENDAR THIS SEASON opens in
Advent, days of expectant waiting, of kindled light bright-
ening against the blanket of darkness that winter brings.
Soon after, Nativity, Holy Birth, Hope and Love cradled in
a straw-strewn manger. And so unfolds the stillness in the
depths of Christmastime. In the Hebrew calendar, too, the
darkness brings the Festival of Light, Hanukkah. One by
one, for eight sweet nights, the oil burns, the wicks are lit.
We are drawn to quietude, keep cacophony at bay. A year
of deepening, of paying attention, of inhaling the Holy has
brought us to blessed stillness as the Sacred anoints our
every hour.

Here, fourteen blessings to wrap yourself in the season's
hardest-won gifts—peace, quiet, and the contentment that
feels most like purring.

WINTER SOLSTICE: *As the solstice brings on winter, celebrate the darkness. Make a bonfire or simply light candles. Throw a log in the fireplace, listen to the crackle. Tradition has it that fires are sparked on the longest night to help the sun get its job done. Give thought to the life that's birthed out of darkness.*

BLESSING 2: *Savor the winter's dawn especially, in all its stillness. Not a leaf fluttering, not a blue jay's squawk or sparrow's chirp. Listen for the still, small voice that's best attended to when quiet at last envelops us.*

BLESSING 3: *We have watched, for weeks now, the slow undressing of the world beyond the sill. There is no hiding in the depth of winter. We battle back darkness with the kindling of the lights, and the stringing of branches with all the glitter we can gather. Look within for truest light.*

BLESSING 4: *Spying the brown-paper packages, tied up in red-plaid ribbons, all stacked under the fir tree, put thought to Elizabeth Barrett Browning's certainty: "God's gifts put man's best dreams to shame."*

CHRISTMAS DAY (DEC. 25): *On the morn of Nativity, wrap yourself in newborn wonder. Awake before anyone else. Light a candle. Look out the window and quietly count your blessings.*

BOXING DAY (DEC. 26): *Quiet and dark are invited in, not whisked away, come the season of stillness. Be hushed. Punctuate your afternoon's walk with a trail of birdseed sprinkled from winter-coat pockets. Take supper by the fire—or near a cove of candles. Fuel on simple soup and sturdy bread. Read stories by firelight. Tuck children in their beds, while grown-ups keep vigil deep into the night.*

BLESSING 7: *Be blanketed in the holy lull that is the first snowfall.*

BLESSING 8: *Revel in the child's joys of deep-freeze winter: Candy canes and marshmallows populating steamy mugs of hot cocoa, the only hope for luring frost-nipped limbs in from out-of-doors. Consider it sweetened invitation to deepened conversation.*

BLESSING 9: *"I love the dark hours of my being / for they deepen my senses . . . / From them I've come to know that I have room / for a second life, timeless and wide."—Rainer Maria Rilke, Bohemian-Austrian poet (1875–1926).*

BLESSING 10: *Morning incantations at the cookstove: Stir a pot of oatmeal—bejeweled with dried fruits from the pantry— for the people we love, still tucked under the covers. Blanket each dreamer in blessings for the day, as you draw the spoon through bubbling porridge.*

BLESSING 11: *Survival seed, you might call it. Imbued with animation and sparks of magic, surely. Not a minute after it's been dumped, the yard's aswirl with sound and stirrings. On days of arctic chill, it's the least we can do, to stoke the hearts and bellies of the birds who give flight to the day, who fill the boughs and branches with their scarlet feathers.*

BLESSING 12: *Pick up a well-thumbed copy of Mary Oliver's* Red Bird, *and drink in her rare brand of poetry.*

BLESSING 13: *Delight in the winged thespians of winter: Keep watch on the flurry of winter's birds coming in for a landing at the feeder, taking turns, shooshing each other away. Ponder this: "Birds are a miracle because they prove to us there is a finer, simpler state of being which we may strive to attain." —Douglas Coupland, Canadian novelist.*

NEW YEAR'S EVE (DEC. 31): *"Don't ask what the world needs. Ask yourself what makes you come alive and go out and do that, because what the world needs is people who have come alive." —Howard Thurman, author, theologian, civil rights leader (1899–1981)*

COUNTING THE DAYS
On Leaning toward the Light

I AM PRACTICING ADVENT. REALLY PRACTICING. Paying attention. Giving in to the season in ways that wash over me, seep into me, bring me back home to a place I may never have been.

Like a child this year, I have a just-opened sense of these days.

I am, for the very first time, not counting down. Not ticking off days and errands to run like a clock wound too tightly.

Instead, I am counting in a whole other way. I am counting, yes, but the thing that I'm doing is making count each one of the days.

I am counting the days in a way that takes time. That takes it and holds it. Savors it. Sucks out the marrow of each blessed hour.

I am this year embracing the darkness. I am kindling lights. I am practicing quiet. I am shutting out noise, and filling my house with the sounds of the season that call me.

I am practicing no. *No* is the word that I'm saying to much of the madness. No, I cannot go there. No, I cannot race from one end of town to the other. No, I will not.

December Field Notes: In this darkest month, when the solstice marks the sun's lowest point in the year, and night stretches

I am practicing yes.

Yes, I will wake up early. Will tiptoe alone, and in quiet, to down in the kitchen, and out to the place where the moon shines. Where the early bird hasn't yet risen. But I have. I am alone with the dark and the calm, and I am standing there watching the shadows, the lace of the moon. I am listening for words that fill up my heart. It's a prayer and it comes to me, fills my lungs, as I breathe in cold air, the air of December, December's most blessed breath.

Yes, I am redressing my house. I am tucking pinecones and berries of red, in places that not long ago were spilling with pumpkins and walnuts and acorns.

I am waking up to the notion that to usher the season into my house is to awaken the sacred. It is to shake off the dust of the days just before. To grope for the glimmer amid all the darkness.

December, more than most any month, can go one of two ways.

One trail is all tangled, all covered with bramble. You can get lost, what with all of the noise and all of the bright colored lights.

But December, if you choose, if you allow it, can be the trail through the woods that leads to the light, far off in the distance.

The darkness itself offers the gift. Each day, the darkness comes sooner, comes deeper, comes blacker than ink. It draws us in, into our homes, yes, but more so, into our souls.

It invites us: Light a light. Wrap a blanket. Sit by the fire. Stare into the flames, and onto the last dying embers. Consider the coming of Christmas.

---

to its longest, ancient peoples feared the solar light might never be kindled again. Back in pagan Scandinavia, Nordic

I am, in this month of preparing, in this month of a story told time and again, listening anew to the words. I am considering the story of the travelers, the Virgin with Child, the donkey, the man with the tools, the unlikely trio, knocking and knocking at door after door.

I am remembering how, long, long ago, I winced when I heard how no one had room. Open the door, I would shout deep inside. Make room. Make a room.

I didn't know then, I could change it. I could take hold of the story; make it be just as it should be.

But I do now. I know now.

I am taking hold of that story, the way that it's told this December. I am, in the dark and the quiet, making the room that I longed for. For the three in the story, yes, but even for me.

I am preparing a room at the inn. The inn, of course, is my heart.

---

merrymakers lit up Juul logs, slugged back mead, tended fires all night long. Romans got downright riotous, decking

THE SOUND OF SNOW FALLING
On the Sanctity of Silence

IT IS DECEMBER'S GIFT.

Whole clouds of it fell last night. Started with a flake or two, barely noticed, in the gray of afternoon. By dinnertime, the boughs, the walks, the feeders for the birds, had lost their definition, were taking on a girth that might have made them groan.

Except the world was wordless.

The world, when I slipped on my snow-exploring shoes, zipped up my puffy coat, was so silenced by the spilling from the sky, I could, without straining, make out the sound of snow falling.

It's a sound, quite truly, that makes your ears perk up. And your soul, too.

Unlike the pit-a-pat of rain, it is wholly unexpected. Wind we know is noisy. Humidity, except for moaning of the ones who find it hard to bear, is not. But that comes as no surprise.

The sound of snow falling, then, is singularly soothing and startling. It is a titillation for the ears, a tickling of the nerves that makes them stand at full attention.

---

halls with rosemary and laurel, burning lamps through the night, carrying on crazily, in hopes of warding off the spirits of

A sound not heard so often, certainly not in months and months, it came like water to a thirsty traveler. And I could not get enough.

There is a stillness in the first of every winter's snow that feels to me like coming home. It is in that unrippled place, that place where quiet is complete and whole, that I, and maybe you, feel as if the hand of God is reaching down, is showing me the way through snowy woods.

Sometimes, too, I think I hear the sound of God, putting gentle finger to soft lips, shushing.

Shhhhhhh, I hear God say. *Be still.*

What else, I wonder, could slow a world that can't move fast enough? Who else can keep the cars off the road? The cell phones from incessant baying?

There was not a soul outside last night, not when I was there at least, and I was there for quite a while.

This morning, then, is quiet squared.

Not even snow is making sound.

It is December's gift, this early snow. It is just in time to serve its highest purpose. To shush a world in full staccato. To make us perk our ears, to see if, this blessed day, we might hear the song of snow falling.

---

darkness. And the Incas went so far as to try to tie the sun to a hitching post, a great stone column, to keep it from escaping

BEING STILL
On Holiness Unfolding

CURIOUS THING THIS DECEMBER, MORE THAN EVER, it is the stillness that speaks to me. That I seek. That some days I grope toward as if blind and making my way through the woods on nothing more than the steadiness of my footsteps and the fine-grained whorl of my fingertips rubbing up against the underbrush, telling me I've lost my way.

It is as if the deep dark stillness itself is divining me toward home.

Which, of course, it is. It always is.

Oh, there's noise all right this December. Clanging like a cymbal in my ear, the squawking from the news box, the screeching of the brakes.

But I am—in my best moments—pushing it away.

I take it in in stiff long drinks—the news, the noise, the grave distractions—but then I do odd things: I lift the blinds at night so I can watch the snowflakes tumbling. I wind the clock and listen

---

*altogether. Nowadays, trusting in the dawn, we needn't be afraid. Rather, longest night beckons quietude. * Full Cold*

183

to its mesmerizing tick and tock. I sit, nose pressed to frosty pane of glass, and watch the scarlet papa cardinal peck at berries on the bough.

I am practicing the art of being still.

Stillness, when you look for it, is never far away, and not too hard to grasp.

I find, though, it takes a dose of concentration. And sometimes a stern reminder; I mumble to myself, "Be still now."

It is Advent, the counting-down time, the something-coming time of darkest winter. And, in my good spells, I am deeply, urgently, savoring the getting there.

I am hauling out my usual armament of soothers and elixirs. I simmer spices on the stove. I scatter corn on drifts of snow. I kindle candle flame. Crank soulful Christmas tunes. Tiptoe down the stairs in deep quietude of night, and stumble onto moonlight making magic out of blue-white undulations in the yard.

I am even dropping to my knees, or curling up in bed with incantations on my lips. They carry me to sleep some nights; what better lullaby?

I am ever thankful this December for the one bright side to all the fiscal downturn: There will be little shopping this year. No running here to there.

I will simply look the ones I love squarely in the eye. I will tell them how deeply and dearly I depend on their presence in my every blessed day.

It is an Advent this year of simple things: There is a ring of candles on the kitchen table, one new one lit each and every week,

---

Moon, or Long Night Moon, lights the long, long night. Even more so, because with the sun so low across the sky, winter

till at December's peak there will be a rising cloud of incandescence as we join our hands and pray.

There is a string of red-plaid pockets, each one numbered, 1 to 24, strung from one window to another, and every single morning, my little one rushes down the stairs to find the sweet tucked there inside the number of the day.

It is, as it so often is, my littlest one who softens me, who stirs me back to stillness, who insists we not forget to give the twisty fir its drink. Who takes me by the hand. Who asks his big, wise brother if he too "checked Advent" (meaning did he yet dig out *his* daily dose of duly-numbered sweet).

It is, nearly as deeply, the thick meringue of snow bending all the branches. It is the flash of scarlet feather at the window. It is the sound of orange peel simmering. And the tinkling of the spoon scraping at the bottom of the cocoa-filled mug.

These are the things that make for stillness, or rather are the keys on the ring that might unlock it after all.

It is, in fact, the heart, the soul, that are the vessels of pure true stillness: those chambers deep inside us that allow for the holy to unfold. The birthing rooms, perhaps, of our most essential stirrings.

To be at one with all that matters. To begin the pulse-beat there where the quiet settles in and the knowing reigns.

It is, yes, in the stillness that the sacred comes.

And this December, more than ever, I am blessed to find it's that, simply surely that, that is carrying me through this tangled woods.

---

*moon arcs higher, and takes longer than during the rest of the year to cross the night sky. * The guiding star in this night sky*

THE PIGEON MAN OF LINCOLN SQUARE
On Saints among Us

THE POLICE CALLED ME LAST NIGHT. A FEW TIMES.

They were calling because an old man, an old, bent-over man, one with a black canvas satchel slung over his shoulders, and too-big janitor's pants held up by suspenders, was shuffling along on a sidewalk, beside a busy city street yesterday, a cold December Tuesday, at 2:15 in the afternoon.

Probably, he was headed off to the fire hydrant, the red one just by the bank at Lawrence and Western, where the pigeons, for years now, have counted him one of their flock.

The old man was walking past a bank parking lot when another old man, one driving a Chevy van, pulled out of the lot. He must not have seen him. The man in the van hit the one with the satchel.

The old man died.

The old man was Joe Zeman. But most everyone called him the Pigeon Man of Lincoln Square. The cops couldn't tell who it was. Except for a newspaper story, one laminated, tucked in the

---

is not the biblical star of Bethlehem. Rather, Orion, the hunter, and Gemini, the twins, move to center stage as winter begins.

satchel, one with a little rectangular label up in the corner, scribbled with the words, "For who ever."

Except for that story, one that showed him, in color, feathered with pigeons, one that told *his* story, the cops and the doctors who pronounced him dead at the hospital had no clue who he was.

The Pigeon Man's life was like that. Barely a soul had a clue who he was. Mostly, only the pigeons.

That's why the cops called me. They knew I knew a bit of his story. I wrote the newspaper story they found in his satchel. Two years and three months later, almost to the day, and he still carried it—maybe half a dozen laminated copies of it—wherever he went.

The cops needed someone to call. Needed to know if there was a soul in the world who might care to know what happened to Joe.

There was no one, save for the pigeons. And me.

Here's just a bit of the Pigeon Man's story, the one he carried till he fell down and died:

"Except for the lips, you would think he was made out of stone, the man who sits, hours on end, on the red fire hydrant on Western Avenue, just north of Lawrence, pigeons by the dozens perched on him.

"Pigeons on his head. Pigeons on his shoulders and right down his arms. Pigeons poised on each palm. Pigeons clinging to his chest. Pigeons on his lap. Pigeons on his thighs. Pigeons, of course, perched on each foot.

"The pigeons peck and coo, occasionally flutter their wings. Sometimes even scatter. But not the man, the man is motionless. You might mistake him for a statue.

And all the darkness brings its own reward: a nighttime canvas stitched in deep-sky splendor. Double and triple stars abound,

"Joseph Zeman," seventy-seven when he died, "can sit for hours, barely flinching a muscle," I wrote. "Except for those lips."

I wrote how he cooed right back to the birds. How he kissed them, right on their iridescent necks, flat on the point of their sharp little beaks. How he nuzzled them, rubbed his nose in their wings, the herringbone of feathers all black and charcoal and pewter and white. How he called them by name, his favorites. How he worried when one was missing in action.

I wrote how up in the attic where he lived a few blocks from the hydrant he kept track, in a neat little ledger, of whatever dollar bills might have been slipped in his hand, dropped by the side of his hydrant.

How he used the money for his pigeon supplies, the unpopped popcorn kernels, the bags of white rice, the loaves of Deerfield Farms enriched white bread, the Maurice Lenell oatmeal cookies, the plain old birdseed that comes in fifty-pound sacks, which he broke down, each night, into zip-top plastic bags.

I wrote too, because he took me up to his attic, because he was proud to show off his deeply thought method, of the old baby food jars he filled, each morning and night, with rice or popcorn, seven jars in all, and tucked in his satchel, each time he shuffled off to the hydrant.

Twice a day, at least, once in the morning, once in the late afternoon, the Pigeon Man returned to his roost.

But the part of the story that's stayed with me all these years was the part where he explained why he was drawn to the pigeons.

"All my life I had so much backstabbing at home, real problems

---

each a celestial wonder—among the most glorious of the as-tronomical calendar. * It's not all ice and snow blanketing crust there. I got to love the animals more, so trustworthy. Fifty years, all I heard was, 'Shut up, shut up.' I needed help at home 'cause I was handicapped. They took advantage of me. Epileptic fits since the day I was born.

"Because I had so much trouble at home, I learned not to say nothing, keep to myself. So they came up to me [the pigeons]; I appreciated the friendship out of a bird more than a person. They're wordless. They come up with pure appreciation."

Zeman, who for forty-seven years ran a newsstand in downtown Chicago, said that he considered sitting on the hydrant the most important work he had ever done.

"I'm really advertising to the public how easy it is to be good without an attitude; it's just as easy to show decency as it is to hate today."

Zeman, a man without much schooling, understood how when he took to the hydrant, raised both his arms, palms upward—the veneration pose, really—as thousands of cars and trucks and smoke-spewing city buses rumbled by, drivers craning their necks to take in the sight of the stooped little man covered in pigeons, he really did resemble a modern-day St. Francis of a city.

Matter of fact, up in his little attic, he had boxes and boxes of St. Francis postcards, each one printed with the peacemaker's prayer: "Lord, make me an instrument of your peace. Where there is hatred, let me sow love . . ."

Matter of fact, Zeman once grabbed a stack of the postcards, maybe a hundred or so, and gave them to me. I tucked them all in the drawer of my desk, here where I do all my typing. I keep

of Earth; rainy season begins in the Pacific Northwest. And
woods aren't wholly barren, with sumac and bittersweet berries

them, right there, to remind me of the wisdom of the lost soul who found his peace with the pigeons.

Just yesterday afternoon, before the phone rang, before any cops called to ask what I knew, I had reached in my drawer for a calculator, and my hand ran into the stack, spilled and scattered, making a mess in the old pine rectangular drawer.

I started to shove the cards back into a stack, but then, for some reason, I picked up the top one, and I read it through to the very last line, which just happens to be, "and it is in dying that we are born to eternal life."

Thinking back on the day, I know that the clock ticking beside me had to have been sliding toward just after two in the afternoon.

That was the hour when the Pigeon Man of Lincoln Square breathed his last breath.

That was the hour the great gray raincloud of pigeons, the ones who for nearly ten years had kept watch on the hydrant, had fluttered down as soon as a little stooped man slid off his satchel, settled onto his cold metal roost, raised both his arms, palms upward—the pose of St. Francis—that was the hour the birds must have let out a most mournful coo.

This morning, for almost the first time in a decade, the hydrant is empty. The pigeons are perched. But the little man with the gentlest heart is not coming.

Not ever again, amen.

---

staying ripe through the winter, ready fuel for the famished. Bald eagles soar in from up north, for milder overwintering.

THE LITTLEST MANGER
On Embracing the Holy Whisper

I LIFTED BABY JESUS out of his tangle of old, old shredded papers. Mary, too. And Joseph, who carries a lantern the size of a fat grain of basmati.

For all the commotion it took to get to them—the ladder that unfolds from the attic had to be pulled, which meant all the boxes in the upstairs hall had to be moved, then I needed a tall someone to help haul down the big cardboard box, the one marked "BAM Merry Christmas," and while I was at it, I noticed the attic needed some shuffling of stuff, which meant that by the time I climbed down the creaky stiff ladder, the one with the joint that might be arthritic, what with its resistance to bending and all the whining it does, I was chilled to the bone—for all that preamble, I have to admit my Holy Little Family just might be a bit underwhelming. A bit easy to miss.

It's odd perhaps, that I so deeply needed them hauled from the attic. It's not like they're commanding whole stretches of real estate. Not like the mantle is theirs and theirs only.

Great Horned Owls pair up, and fashion love songs as they do so. Chipmunks go underground for the long winter's nap. But

As a matter of fact, they are tucked right on the ledge of a birdhouse I ferried home from a farm a few summers ago. Tossed it in the back of a pickup, watched it bounce down a long country road. It's a birdhouse built to look like the church on the top of the hill in that sweet farmer town, and, now, it's the perch for my Holiest Littlest Family.

I was practically hungry for the three tiny folk to get out of the box where I lay them each year when it's time to put away Christmas. I was hungry in that way when your soul is silently growling. Like when your tummy needs soup, only this is your soul, and it needs sustenance too.

That little manger—for something ninety-nine folks out of a hundred might walk right past, not even notice—is, like all symbol in life, packed with a wallop of meaning to me.

It is my whole Christmas distilled. It is the essence of a very long journey. It tells the story of a Christian and a Jew, of a life and a love that was never imagined.

The Christian is one who once saw the hand of God everywhere. Once watched, through spread fingers and tears from a pew in a nunnery chapel, as the face of Jesus up on the Cross changed like a Kodak slide show, all kinds of faces—black and brown, wrinkled and gray, a dozen or so, a true tour of the world, in faces—a miracle that spoke in the most certain words: Find God in each and every face.

The Jew in this story is deeply observant, bore his own heartache marrying outside of the tribe. Outside of the lines, he colored his life.

---

fox and gray squirrel fancy all the roaming room, and make the best of it with Mother Nature's call to mate.

They both did.

The question that's posed, and answered, in that small wood-carved trio is this: How in a home—how in the sacred space you build only on trust and faith in each other's capacity to move beyond what you've known all your lives—how do you weave together the Christmas that means everything with the one that always was cast as a threat to your people, your race, and religion?

I started small. I started on tiptoes.

There is no place in my heart or my home for bombast or noise. Certainly not trickery. I am wrenched, frankly, when I read of interfaith families who use Christmas and Hanukkah as some sorts of weapons, a tug-of-war rope to see whose holiday is left standing, and whose falls. I did not marry a man I love, did not nosedive out of the safe zone, to whittle away my life playing holiday games.

And so, amid a whole carton of hand-me-down wooden carved angels and shepherds and even a platoon of brass-playing penguins, long ago on our very first Christmas, I moved back the tangle of old paper shreds, and there lay Baby Jesus, a toppled Joseph, and upturned Mary, as well.

I remember catching my breath, gasping, and staring at the sweet little family. I lifted each one in my palm.

I knew then, that very first Christmas, that I had a crèche I could softly, quietly, tuck off to the side. Wouldn't ruffle a feather. Wouldn't stir, not even a mouse.

The fact of the interfaith journey is that—if you are paying attention, if you are listening closely—it can be a long, arid road. You might spend a few years in the desert. You might fall on your knees, night after night, praying one thing: Dear God, keep the pilot light lit. Don't let it snuff out.

The fact of the interfaith Christmas is you need to be gentle. Need to listen with very big ears to the layers of history. You need to know that a tree isn't only a tree. A tree, when you grew up Jewish, was one thing that separated you from all of your neighbors. You were proud of that fact. It meant, you believed, that you were the people God chose. It meant, too, you were the people painfully persecuted. By Christians as well as the Nazis. At separate times, in separate ways, but persecuted nonetheless.

Never once have we not gotten a tree. My husband, God bless him, has joyfully carried one home, year after year. Last year, he grabbed the fattest one on the lot. Fraser fir, too, the best that there is in the Christmas tree business.

A crèche, though, I feared, might be pushing a little too far. So I joyfully settled my heart into the littlest one that came in the box.

It's always been my own little Christmas. My devotion was quiet, was whispered, was in the deep of the night. Or when everyone else in the house had magically vanished, and I was alone.

It carried me through years of not knowing, of finding my way through this uncharted forest. For a few years there, for a whole host of reasons, my ironclad knowing had been shaken and shattered. I was left holding little but shards.

Still, Christmas came all those years. And I clung to my Littlest Manger. My manger that didn't get in the way, that no one needed to notice. But that held me, rapt.

And then, not long ago, I somehow got to the summit. I realized the power of story, regardless of provable fact.

In the utterly simple, deeply profound truth of the matter, I took in the whole Christmas story for the power of its infinite metaphor: a babe born in a barn; the unlikely virgin mother; the carpenter guardian; the chorus of barnyard critters; the innkeepers who hadn't a room; the bright shining light in the heavens; the shepherds and journeying kings.

For a minute there I thought maybe I needed to find myself a crèche bigger than the tips of my fingers. Thought, really, it's time to not tiptoe.

But then, I lifted my littlest manger from out of the box. And I realized how perfect it is for the Christmas I believe in with all of my heart: It is Christmas condensed to its delicious, delectable best.

It is Christmas in whispers. It is a babe born in the night. It is a Savior whose very first cry was let out in the straw of a barn. It is the Lord, greeted by shepherds.

And that is a story I am blessed to call mine.

WHEN WONDER COMES FOR CHRISTMAS
On Solitude and Oneness
under Heaven's Dome

WHEN AT LAST THE MORNING COMES, I am not unlike the little child at Christmas. Having tossed and turned in anticipation, through all the darkest hours, at first light I throw back the blankets, slide into clogs, slither into a heavy sweater, and tiptoe down the stairs.

For days, I've been stockpiling for my friends. I've corncakes stuffed with cranberries and pinecones wrapped in peanut butter. I've suet balls to dangle from the boughs, and little bags of birdseed, just small enough to stuff in all my pockets. I've a jug of fresh water for all to drink and splash before it turns to winter's ice.

It's time for a Christmas treasure all my own, one I unwrap every year.

My walk of wonder takes me no farther than the patch of earth I call my own, a rather unassuming tangle of hope and dreams and heartache (for what garden doesn't crack a heart, at least once a season?), in my leafy little village.

I carve out this hour of Christmas morn, before the footsteps slap across the floorboards up the stairs, before I crank the stove, and kindle all the Christmas lights.

It's my hour of solitude and near silence, as I tug open the back door and step into the black-blue darkness of the minutes just beyond the dawn.

It's my chance to take in the winter gifts of my rambling, oft-rambunctious garden plots, and all who dwell among them—the birds, the squirrels, and fat-cheeked chipmunks, the old mama possum, and, yes, the stinky skunk who sometimes ambles by and sends us dashing in all directions.

And, best of all, it's my early Christmas moment to reciprocate the many gifts that all the seasons bring me.

I am nearly humming as I make my Yuletide rounds: I fill the feeders, scatter seed, and stuff an old stone trough with what I call the "critter Christmas cakes."

At this scant hour, the black-velvet dome above is stitched still with silver threads of sparkling light. And limbs of trees, bare naked in December, don't block my upward glance at all that heavens offer.

This is where my prayer begins, as I whisper thanks for all the chirps and song, for flapping wings and little paws that scamper—all of nature's pulse beats that bring endless joy, and teach eternal lessons.

As light brightens in the southeast corner of the sky, the architecture of the wintry bower emerges. The black of branches—some gnarled, others not unlike the bristles of an upturned broom—etch sharp against the ever-bluer sky.

Exposed, the silhouette reveals the secrets of the trees—the oak, the maple, and the honey locust that rustles up against my bedroom window.

As I come round a bend, gaze up and all around, I cannot miss the nests not seen till late in autumn, when the trees disrobed and shook off their blazing colors.

In murky morning light, the nests appear as inkblots of black among the lacy boughs. Only in winter do we realize how many dot the arbor. There is the contour of the squirrels' shoddy leaf-upholstered hovel high up in the maple, and, down low in a serviceberry, the robins' tuck-point masterpiece of twigs.

While in robust and leafy times, the trees did not let on, but in winter's stripped-down state there's no hiding the part they play in watching over the nursery, shielding barely feathered broods and not-yet-furry baby squirrels from wind and sleet and pounding rains. Or even too much sun.

This cold morning, all is still. Every nest is empty, every birdhouse hollow once again. Where the winter birds cower, where they huddle, close their eyes and doze, I cannot figure out. Somewhere, even at this illuminating hour, they're tucked away in slumber.

It won't be long till the stirrings come, but for now the only sound is the scritch-scratch of brambles and left-behind leaves as they brush against my legs. I make my way among them, along a bluestone path, past all the shriveled blooms of not-forgotten summer.

The moppy heads of hydrangea, now dried and crisped to brown, are bowed but not surrendered, still clinging, even in the cold. And all that's left of all the roses are persimmon-colored full-to-bursting hips, a final exhortation, punctuation on the winter page.

By the time the Big Dipper fades from the morning sky, that early riser, papa cardinal, ignites the winterscape with his scarlet coat. Soon follows the red-bellied woodpecker, a nuthatch or two, and, not long after, the choristers of dun-robed sparrows, all a-chatter with Christmas morning news.

I take cover back behind a fir tree, where the crowd at the feeder pays no mind. And where in winter storms, I find the flocks, too, take shelter, the only branches left that promise shield and a place to hunker down. For anyone who wants to hide—too often it's the hungry hawk—these piney limbs are plenty thick.

Then I get brazen, and toss a handful of peanuts to the bristle-tailed squirrels. These are mere hors d'oeuvres, of course, for that trough now spills with Dickensian plenty—among the larder, bumpy apples no one wanted, and pumpkins plucked from the after-Thanksgiving discount bin.

It is all my way of making real my unending gratitude, of bowing deep and soulfully to Blessed Mama Earth.

FROM THE WINTER
Recipe Box

A Christmas Gift . . .

Christmas-Eve Elves' French Toast . . .

It's been tradition, long as I can remember, that, come Christmas morn, I'm first one out from under the bed-sheets. I've been known to take two steps at a leap, to plug in the tree, and get to work in the kitchen. For years, that meant Christmas-y coffeecake, a la page 337 of the highly-splattered *Silver Palate Good Times Cookbook*. But then I enlisted the Christmas Eve elves. In short, their magic trick is this: overnight soak, swift slide in the oven, and—poof!—rising cloud of cinnamon, yolk, and butter. Suddenly, I discovered more time for sitting alone under the tree. And, with far less fuss, the vapors seeping from the oven smelled just as get-out-of-bed as that yeasty rise, on a morning when eager boys need little stirring to spring from under the covers. It's pure prestidigitation, too, on any snowy morn, when those who snooze in your beds need an extra dollop of oomph to arise and seize the day.

Provenance: Inspired by a long-ago recipe in the Chicago Tribune, *though my own fiddling at the cookstove might make this unrecognizable from the original.*

Yield: One 9-by-13 casserole

1 loaf challah (the braided egg bread, or whatever holiday loaf strikes your fancy), cut into eight 1-inch-thick slices, or however many snugly fit your 9-by-13 baking dish

2 cups whole milk

1 cup cream (it's Christmas, after all)

8 large eggs

4 tsps. sugar

1 tbsp. best vanilla extract

Few shakes cinnamon

1 orange, grated (if you're so inspired)

3/4 tsp. salt

1/2 cup dried fruits (the jeweled bits of garnet cranberries, plump apricots, make the bake dressed-up enough for Christmas)

2 tbsps. butter, cut into small pieces

Powdered sugar, for dusting

Maple syrup, honey, or your best Christmas-y jam

* Generously butter 9-by-13-inch baking dish.

* Layer bread slices across bottom of dish so it's completely covered, and filled to the top.

* In separate bowl, mix milk, cream, eggs, sugar, vanilla, cinnamon, orange rind, and salt in large bowl.

* Pour over bread. Toss in a handful of dried fruits, tucking in between and under bread slices.

* Cover with foil.

* Refrigerate, covered overnight. (This is where the Christmas-Eve elves come in.)

* Next morning, preheat oven to 350-degrees Fahrenheit.

* Remove egg-cream-bread heavenliness from refrigerator and uncover; it's not necessary to bring casserole to room temperature. Dot top with butter.

* Bake uncovered, until puffed and golden, 45 to 50 minutes.

* Let stand 5 minutes before serving.

* Dust with powdered sugar, and serve with maple syrup, honey, jam, or whatever sweet stokes your sugarplum dreams.

Merry, merry, but of course . . .

ACKNOWLEDGMENTS

IN MY GESTATIONAL HISTORY, I'VE BIRTHED TWO BABIES, miscarried three. Writing a book certainly feels gestational—only this time, as the author, I actually got to choose how to sequence the compositional DNA, the words.

The birth of a book, honestly, begins long before the first keystrokes. To be ready to write, to have the depth from which to draw, there must have been guardian angels and believers along the way. Too often, they never know the difference they made, the imprint they left, the windows they opened. In my life, the guardian angels who brought me to the moment of this book include Lou Crouch, Gertrude Gutting, Tasha Tudor, Gracie Tynan, Paige Williams, Dorothy Denzler, MB Williams, Sheila Wolfe, Charles Leroux, John Teets, Nancy Watkins, Renee Enna, Elizabeth Taylor, Mark Burrows, Elwyn Brooks White, Mary Oliver. And of course, my mama, papa, and four far-flung brothers, especially Brian, my on-demand tech coach.

The art of midwifery is intimate, involves entering the pain, encouraging the push, and always believing in the miracle ending. The midwives who huddled close as I crafted this book include Lil Copan and Lauren Winner, and the team at Abingdon Press (Julie Gwinn, most emphatically), and, on the home front, Blair Kamin, who generously read and inked and critiqued. With unswerving grace, they pulled me through to the moment the cry went up in the delivery room.

But, hovering in that hallowed room, a cadre of angels to whom I owe the deepest gratitude, and a rare brand of love: Linda Lewis, Ann Marie Lipinski, and my mother-in-law, Virginia Kamin, who has always, always believed there was a book.

All my life I've gathered "sisters," and without them I'd be a wobbly mess: Becca Neumann, Cheryl Devall, Mary Mullane Mittelbach, and, not least, my "sisters" from Pull Up a Chair, a loyal and breathtaking circle if ever there was one. My cookery sisters, Brooke Kamin Rapaport and Susan Faurot, define deliciousness. And I am forever blessed by two bravest of women, Susan Loeb and Katie Seigenthaler, whose magnificent ever-tender hearts are among my life's treasures. As is Jan Sugar, who keeps me afloat with her all-purpose excellence.

Writerly lights of my life, Jen B. McDonald and Betsy O'Donovan, along with Nadia Tromp and the sisterhood of Niemans; thank you for illuminations without end.

Woven into these pages are the countless snippets of paper, and underlined words, and the hundreds of dog-eared books crammed onto my library shelves—the collected astonishments and wonders of a girl who grew up inhaling words, the way anybody else might gobble down chocolate. To the logophiles who shared the delight and stoked the steady diet, blessings.

Most of all, these pages would be blank if not for the loves and joys of my life—the two boys I birthed, and who in many ways birthed the best of me—Sweet Will and Teddy. And to their most blessed father, the one who, every day, puts the wind beneath my wings, Blair Kamin, a lifetime of thank you.

And to the God who never left, I stand in open-hearted awe. May I ever be your pencil.

NOTES

Epigraph
"Praying: It doesn't have to be the blue iris . . ."
Mary Oliver, "Praying," in *Thirst* (Boston: Beacon Press, 2006), 37. Used herewith by permission of the Charlotte Sheedy Literary Agency, Inc.

Winter: Deepening
Field Notes
All field notes are compiled through a vast stack of sources, including but not limited to Paul Ehrlich, David S. Dobkin, and Darryl Wheye, *The Birder's Handbook: A Field Guide to the Natural History of North American Birds* (New York: Simon & Schuster, 1988); Donald and Lillian Stokes, *Stokes Field Guide to Birds* (Boston: Little, Brown and Company, 1996); Bill Laws, *The Field Guide to Fields* (Washington, D.C.: National Geographic, 2010); Mark R. Chartrand, *National Audubon Society Field Guide to the Night Sky* (New York: Alfred A. Knopf, 1991); Old Farmer's Almanac, www.almanac.com/; Sky & Telescope: The Essential Guide to Astronomy, www.skyandtelescope.com/. Particularly illuminating, the esteemed astronomers and historians at the Adler Planetarium in Chicago, always generous with their vast knowledge of the heavens.

"We have come to this hallowed spot . . ."
Rev. Dr. Martin Luther King, Jr., "I Have a Dream," Aug. 28, 1963, speech transcription, 2–4. Copyright held by the Estate of Martin Luther King, Jr., Inc. Full text PDF found at http://www.thekingcenter.org/archive/document/i-have-dream-1

Spring: Quickening
"Lord, That I May See!"
Caryll Houselander, *The Way of the Cross* (Ligouri, MO: Liguori Publications, 2002), 6. Adapted by St. Nicholas Church, Evanston, IL.

"Drive me by the strength of your tenderness . . ."
Houselander, 47–48.

"Holes are created in time . . ."
Gertrud Mueller Nelson, *To Dance with God: Family Ritual and Community Celebration* (Mahwah, NJ: Paulist Press, 1986), 28–29.

"The gods, taking pity on mankind . . ."
Nelson, 29.

"the very act which makes the transition . . ."
Nelson, 29.

Summer: Plenitude
"audible stillness"
Nathaniel Hawthorne, "From an Old Manse," in *Mosses from an Old Manse*, ed. George Parsons Lathrop (Boston: Houghton Mifflin & Co., 1883), 22.

"But there is still one more thing . . ."
Barbara Cooney, *Miss Rumphius* (New York: Viking Penguin, Inc., 1982), 15.

"All that summer . . ."
Cooney, 21.

"In this hour divinely fresh . . ."
Celia Thaxter, *An Island Garden* (Boston: Houghton Mifflin & Co., 1894), 112–13.

"People are like stained-glass windows . . ."
Elisabeth Kubler-Ross, "Life and Death: Lessons from the Dying," in *To Live and To Die: When, Why, and How*, ed. Robert Hardin Williams (New York: Springer-Verlag, 1973), 150.

Autumn: Awe
the sword's flash
Ann Druitt, Christine Fynes-Clinton, Marije Rowling, *All Year Round* (Stroud, Gloucestershire, UK: Hawthorn Press, 1995), 139.

"being completely absorbed in the love of God . . ."
Thomas of Celano quoted in Arnaldo Fortini, *Francis of Assisi*, trans. Helen Helen Moak (New York: The Crossroad Publishing Company, 1981), 534.

"intelligent of seasons"
John Milton, *Paradise Lost* in Thomas Newton, Charles Dunster, and Thomas Warton, *The Poetical Works of John Milton: With Notes of Various Authors, to which is prefixed Newton's Life of Milton, Vol. 2* (Oxford: W. Baxter, 1824), VII, 39.

"the wabi-sabi season"
Organic farmer Henry Brockman, of Congerville, IL, is among the most eloquent on the "wabi-sabiness" of harvest time. His sister, a poet-writer, captures his musings in her beautiful memoir: Terra Brockman, *The Seasons on Henry's Farm: A Year of Food and Life on a Sustainable Farm* (Evanston, IL: Agate Surrey, 2009), 54.

"Contemplation is life itself . . ."
Thomas Merton, *New Seeds of Contemplation* (New York: New Directions Press, 1962), 1.

"The bee is the only creature . . ."
Karl von Leoprechting quoted in Hilda M. Ransome, *The Sacred Bee in Ancient Times and Folklore* (orig. London: George Allen & Unwin, 1937; Mineola, NY: Dover, 2004), 155.

. . . opened up the book . . .
Gloria Kaufer Greene, "Lamb and Brown Rice Pilaf," in *The Jewish Holiday Cookbook: An International Collection of Recipes and Customs* (New York: Times Books, 1985), 82–83.

Leviticus, chapter 23
Leviticus 23, Verses 34-36.

Winter: Stillness

Christmas classic
O. Henry, "The Gift of the Magi," my favorite, in Tasha Tudor, *Take Joy!* (Cleveland: Wm. Collins Publishers, 1966), 47–51.

"God's gifts put man's best dreams . . ."
Elizabeth Barrett Browning, "Sonnets from the Portuguese 26: I lived with visions for my company," in *Poems: New Edition*, 2 volumes (London: Chapman & Hall, 1850); republished as *The Poems of Elizabeth Barrett Browning* (New York: C. S. Francis/Boston: J. H. Francis, 1850).

"I love the dark hours of my being . . ."
Rainer Maria Rilke, *Prayers of a Young Poet*, trans. Mark S. Burrows (Brewster, MA: Paraclete Press, 2013), 24.

drink in her rare brand of poetry
Mary Oliver, *Red Bird: Poems* (Boston: Beacon Press, 2008).

"Birds are a miracle . . ."
Douglas Coupland, *Life After God* (New York: Pocket Books, 1994), 80–81.

"Don't ask what the world needs . . ."
Howard Thurman quoted in Gil Bailie, *Violence Unveiled: Humanity at the Crossroads* (New York: The Crossroad Publishing Company, 1995), xv.

"Except for the lips . . ."
Barbara Mahany, "The Pigeon Man of Lincoln Square," *Chicago Tribune* (Sept. 19, 2004): Section 13, 3.

"All my life I had so much backstabbing at home . . ."
Joseph Zeman quoted in Mahany, *Tribune*, 3.

When at last the morning comes
Barbara Mahany, "When wonder comes for Christmas," *Chicago Tribune* (Dec. 25, 2011): Section 6, 6-7. Reprinted with permission of the Chicago Tribune; copyright Chicago Tribune; all rights reserved.

Inspired by a long-ago recipe in the Chicago Tribune
Original *Tribune* recipe not found in the archives, but it's digitalized here: http://www.tastebook.com/recipes/1017882-Oven-French-Toast